CONQUER THE CUSTODY AND VISITATION CASE

R. RAY BROOKS, ESQ.

Torchflame Books
An imprint of Light Messages

For my wonderful wife Elizabeth.

CONTENTS

Preface

There is absolutely no way to put a happy face on this process. The best day that you will have before your custody trial or before you enter into an agreement with your ex-spouse or partner will be a day filled with anxiety, fear and trepidation about the unknown. The costs in legal fees and investigative expenses can be staggering. To make matters worse, no one can give you any guarantees about the ultimate outcome of your custody and visitation case. The best anyone can do is to give you an educated guess. You're really going to have to put your trust in your lawyer's skill and advice. It's something that's really difficult, too, because you just met him or her. However, this is something you have to do for the children, not only for yourself. You must take your ego and your fear of losing them out of the equation and do it solely for your belief that not doing it will cause them harm.

A custody and/or visitation action is one of the only proceedings that I would NEVER advise anyone to take on by themselves either. It is too technical, too emotional, and too full of "land mines." You really need help with this, and I can't stress it too much. You will never be able to learn the nuance of this while you're trying to do it. Additionally, you'll never be able to separate your emotional self from your analytical self long enough or effectively enough to put the proof that you'll need to win a trial. You need an unbiased professional mind to look at this for you to save you from yourself. You will never be able to put on a custody trial without having your emotions and your personal stake in the outcome ruin your presentation. Re-read chapters 1-3 in *Divorce and Conquer* and hire yourself the best custody lawyer you can find and afford.

If you read *Divorce and Conquer*, you know that anyone who tries to give you any guarantee as far as a result on one of these cases is just lying to you. Additionally, you can never really trust a lawyer who gives you a statistical history of his or her accomplishments in court. There are simply too many ways to interpret those results, and too many ways to manipulate the statistics. Many lawyers who tout their own win/loss statistics have simply manipulated them in such a way so as to impress you. The example I usually give is the client whose case involves support, property division, a question of attorney's fees *and* child custody and visitation issues. If that person wins *every* aspect of the trial but loses his or her custody and visitation claim, they will probably consider it a loss. The attorney who spends too much time touting statistics will call that a win because he has won eighty percent of the case. If you lost custody of your kids in court, I suspect you'd call it a loss. See what I mean?

Your family history (or the history within your family) is everything in these cases. You cannot change history, which will control the evidence in these cases, but you can change some facts going forward (what I call *future* history). A great deal of the decision-making process by the judge in your custody and visitation case will be based on history, both past and future. As a matter of fact, a significant number of jurisdictions *require* the judge to "consider the detailed history of the family and its unique facts." This history will be reported and described by witnesses, documents, and experts.

The good news is that much of the history that will be interesting to the judge will be created after your separation from your spouse or co-parent. What you do when you're living apart and you're not the best of friends anymore will give the judge an idea of what you can be expected to do in that *future* history.

A lot of what you will read in this book will be to assist you and guide you in creating that history. In other words, what you do now and before the trial can and will make a difference, in many cases a lot of difference. The fact that you're about to file a divorce or custody action does not mean you can't do a lot to help (or damage) your chances on this.

As I said above, no one can give you any guarantees on the outcome of a custody or visitation trial. This book, however, will act as a guideline on how to maximize and understand the process and the proof needed to win or at the very least give you the optimum chance to win. You *can* change your chances!

Remember, nothing written here should be construed as legal advice. There's no way I can give you legal advice without having met you and listened to the particulars of your situation and family dynamic. Only your attorney can do that. He or she is the one with the training and expertise in your state and your jurisdiction to give you the specific information and guidance that will bring you success or the best chance of it. I can only describe processes to you and hopefully give you an outline to think about and to do every day to put you in a position for success.

Be careful though. If you talk to your lawyer every single day, this process is going to be extremely expensive and your attorney will probably get tired of you relatively quickly. You can, however, use this book as an outline for actions that should be done and a quick reference material for any questions. Remember, if you don't tell your lawyer the whole truth, you may have defeated yourself already.

When I began my practice in 1978, only about one in 500 contesting fathers received custody of the children after a custody trial. Many things were different then. First off, family units in 1978 were significantly different than now. The normal situation was that a man worked and a woman stayed home and took care of the children. Also in 1978, the judges were much different. The vast majority were older gentlemen who had a different view on marriage, divorce, and division of family responsibility. In the intervening 35 years, much has changed. First, many children are born outside of wedlock to parents who either don't live together or have never lived together. Many more women are in the workforce and are career-oriented. The judiciary is significantly younger and in many jurisdictions is fifty percent female. Consequently, the success rate of contesting fathers in custody matters has risen to approximately one in three or four. Thirty-five years ago a man trying to get custody of the kids was almost always engaging in an act of futility. It took very special circumstances for it to happen. Men are much more likely now to be successful in their quest to become or remain the legal custodial parent in the twenty-first century. Both men and women reading this have to understand the environment of the nearly "level playing field" in the new millennium. No one should feel like they have a better chance at success than the other because of their sex anymore. You have to really buckle down and follow the tips in this work and take the advice of your lawyer. Don't expect him or her to do it all for you though. You have to make the *future* history that will convince the judge to make you the primary residential parent or the parent who should have significant extended visitation. Only you can do that.

I'm going to make this paragraph as brief as possible, but you may need a little history. Until the 1700s, divorcing fathers were routinely given the custody of the children. Women were, for the most part considered chattel or possessions. They had little if any standing (right to make requests) in court and didn't vote. English Common Law, from which we get our history, changed in about 1839 (as did ours) to give mothers custody of the children under age seven and to award visiting rights to mothers of children over seven. It was still a man's world in court, however, and there were very few divorces. This gradually evolved to a situation in which mothers received custody of the kids most of the time based on the "bread winner versus housewife" division of responsibilities in the first part of the twentieth century. The Uniform Marriage and Divorce Act of 1970 began to chip away at the unwritten presumptions of giving "Mom" the kids and the "Equal Rights" amendments of the 1970s and 1980s did the rest as far as statutes go. Most states now have specific laws abolishing what were called "tender years" doctrines which gave the mother a greater chance of success with young children, too.

All parents now, whether they're male or female, gay or straight, married or unmarried, have, if not a completely level playing field, one that is much more level. However, this statement comes with a warning. Each judge comes with his or her own set of prejudices and stereotypes. All judges get a reputation among the family law Bar Association for their propensities and the likelihood of success of any given person coming before them. Your lawyer's guidance on this aspect of your trial is going to be indispensable. If you know the judge is reluctant to grant custody of kids to a woman, your lawyer will advise you (if you're a female client) to negotiate as much and as far as you can before you go to court. If the same is true of another judge with a man, the lawyer should advise the man to negotiate as much as possible. Of course, if you have great facts, go for it!

Facts and evidence still remain facts and evidence. You'll have to prove your case. You'll still need advice, guidance, and help to navigate your way through this painful process. Read these pages, listen to your lawyer, and take all the suggestions from both places. If you do, you can be confident that you have given yourself every opportunity to be successful.

Finally, I must apologize in advance for the constant and continued use of words and phrases like "most," "many," "for the most part," "generally," and "the majority" when talking about state laws and rules. The truth is that they're all just a little different from each other and it can't be said that all states do this or that the same way. Sorry!

1

The Basic Jurisdiction Issues and Technical Stuff

This chapter is technical because it has to be. Let me apologize for sticking so closely to "legalese" but in this part there's no real option.

Each individual state and jurisdiction has its own statutes, rules, and procedures for handling child custody matters, but child custody and visitation actions can be commenced whether or not the parties were married or ever even lived together. You do **not** have to be married to file an action for custody or visitation, and you may even be a same sex couple in many jurisdictions.

THE UNIFORM CHILD CUSTODY JURISDICTION AND ENFORCEMENT ACT

The UCCJEA (Uniform Child Custody Jurisdiction and Enforcement Act) was created by the National Conference of Commissioners on uniform state laws originally in 1997. The UCCJEA has been adopted by 49 states, the District of

Columbia, Guam, and the U.S. Virgin Islands. The UCCJEA gives exclusive jurisdiction for custody matters to a child's "home state." The home state is defined as the state where a child has lived with a parent for six consecutive months prior to the commencement of the proceeding (or since birth for children younger than six months). If the child has not lived in any state for at least six months prior to the filing, then a court may take jurisdiction in a state that has (1) significant connections with the child and at least one parent in the state, and (2) substantial evidence concerning the child's care, protection, training, and personal relationships. This is not terribly difficult to understand. The desire is that contesting parents should be prohibited or least discouraged from what's known as "forum shopping." Forum shopping is a process that used to involve contesting parents trying to get jurisdiction in a place that would be more advantageous for them but not necessarily the place where many of the witnesses or evidence might be found. Before the UCCJEA, the courts were faced with conflicting arguments with regard to where the trial should be held. Additionally, there were some cases where the parents might "grab" the kids and take them to a different place or jurisdiction where they would claim the case should be held because that state may have more advantageous laws for that parent (or maybe even an uncle who was a judge).

Now, both the UCCJEA and the Federal Parental Kidnapping Prevention Act prohibit parents from doing that sort of thing. That's right, that last one has criminal sanctions attached to it. You shouldn't even think about it. If you try something like abducting the kids to a different state, you may expose yourself to criminal problems, and you'll surely convince the judge deciding your case that you can't be trusted.

If the child has no state for purposes of jurisdiction under the act, then jurisdiction is determined to be proper where the child and at least one parent have significant connections with the state (other than mere presence) and substantial evidence concerning the custody determination is available (school records, doctors records, etc.).

Once any state has made a custody determination, that state keeps jurisdiction over all matters concerning the child unless (1) the state loses it through the child's relocation for six months or something like that. For a state to lose jurisdiction, however, the facts have to be convincing and may in some cases have to be permanent; (2) the court determines that the child and the parent do not have significant connections with the state anymore and evidence concerning the child's custody determination is not available, or (3) the court determines that the child and both parents or acting parents do not reside in the state any longer. Acting parents could be grandparents or even an uncle or aunt with a custody order.

Once a custody determination has been made, no other state court can have jurisdiction to modify the original court order unless or until the original state with jurisdiction determines that the child or any parents or acting parents reside in another state. In some cases, the parent who has moved to another state and has lived there with the child for a while may petition the new state for jurisdiction. The move to another state would usually have to be either with the consent of the other parent or without the other parent's objection. In case of an emergency, however, another state can exercise jurisdiction when the child is in the state.

The act provides that a state court that does not otherwise have jurisdiction **may** enter a temporary order (emergency) if the child is some immediate danger and needs protection. The order has to provide sufficient time for the parties to go back to the original state of jurisdiction and argue all issues before the court.

This gives you an idea of the origins of your state court's jurisdiction and authority to issue orders on child custody. I know this is pretty dry and technical stuff, but believe me when I tell you that volumes of case law have been written determining the meaning of these words as well as their importance and applicability to specific cases. It's pretty rare these days that a jurisdictional argument happens. When it does, it's usually in cases where one parent has taken the child or children to another state temporarily but then tries to use the act to claim jurisdiction, or there could be an attempt after a significant amount of time (five months?) to say that the child's significant contacts with the former state are not as strong or as current as the state now proposed as having jurisdiction.

The really tough situations occur when the parties agree that the child will live with one parent or other on a temporary basis which turns in to six months or more. Parents who live and work in different jurisdictions could find themselves in the situation.

In most states every custody action requires the party beginning the action, and in some places the responsive party, to fill out the uniform child custody jurisdiction act affidavit before the action can be commenced. I've attached one of these at the end of this work so that you can see the sorts of things you have to be able to swear to before you can even bring a custody action. Again, you don't have to be in a divorce case to invoke the jurisdiction of the court. You can file a simple custody matter without divorce as among unmarried parents or even domestic partners.

Please don't think that there can't be arguments about the interpretation of these things. Smart, innovative legal minds can differ about the interpretation of all of this stuff. Each individual case is going to have to be analyzed by the attorney handling it to know how to proceed. Ultimately, when the jurisdictional argument comes up, a judge will have to decide whether your case fits the description of facts that gives jurisdiction to your state court or not. You shouldn't worry about this too much, however. The vast majority of cases filed don't have state-to-state jurisdictional arguments.

2

What Kinds of Time Sharing Schedules Are There?

The types and kinds of time sharing schedules are as varied and as different as you or the judge can make them. The very first consideration that you should have in the beginning of this process is to realistically look at who you are, who your co-parent is, what the parenting dynamic has been during the course of your relationship, and what you expect that parenting dynamic to be after you separate.

You should make a realistic evaluation as to what you can achieve in terms of time sharing with a look toward what your circumstances will be like when you're living on your own and your ex is living on his or her own. If financial considerations dictate that you're going to be living in a small apartment after the separation and after the process is over, you should really consider whether that small apartment setting is going to be something that's good for the kids to live in on a day-to-day basis. If your family has had the home place for a while and you're the one staying in it, you're going to be in a better position than the person leaving the home place as far as the residential situation goes.

For the most part, circumstances dictate who stays and who goes, but there could be an argument about who stays in the family home as part of the divorce or custody action. Remember, at times the judge can award use and possession of the home as part of a custody, visitation, and support final judgment. Frankly it's not terribly uncommon for a judge to do that. If circumstances dictate that you both move out of the home, make sure the new apartment or new home is a good place for kids to spend time and possibly grow up. No judge is terribly happy about awarding children to a partner who plans to move again or moves on a regular basis. We'll talk more about that later.

You should also evaluate what your life is going to be like after you're single again and what kind of time you're going to have to devote to raising the kids or just spending time with them. A lot of people go into this process insisting on having the title "primary residential parent" without really thinking what that means. Think for a moment about the last time you were left alone with the kids for a week or two weeks while your partner had to go away on business or went away fishing with his buddies or went on a girl's trip some place. You had the responsibility for the kids 24 hours a day. You have to think of their needs, wants, and obligations even before you think of yours. Are you prepared to do that for the rest of the time the kids live in your house? Is your job such that you can be available every afternoon to take care of the kids after school? Would you have the option of taking off work early to pick up a sick or injured child at school and spend the rest of the day in a doctor's office or at home? Think it over. If you're a classic type "A" who routinely spends 60 hours per week in the office, or who is on call at night, or the person who doesn't know who the kids' pediatrician or dentist is, it may be an idea to reevaluate your wants and what you think is right for the kids. No one is saying that type "A" personalities can't be good parents. It's just that, probably in the past, your career has taken a front seat and the family maybe in a back seat. Are you willing to stop now and turn into somebody else?

Are you interested in starting a new social life? Having kids 24 hours a day does not leave an awful lot of time for starting a new relationship. It can be done, but remember if you have the kids 24 hours a day, when are you going to spend time with the new relationship? You can't introduce the kids to everybody you're dating, so you can't bring them home. This means that you're going to be spending time away from the children. Is this something that you can plan on and still have the kids 24 hours a day?

The point is that you have to be realistic about what you expect your life to be like after the separation and after the final hearing. You also have to remember that if you go through a contested custody and visitation battle, your ex may not be as happy to work with you on trading off times with the kids as he or she might have been in the past. He or she will be starting life over too, and may not be terribly willing to give you a break, particularly if you need the break to start a new relationship.

Try to imagine yourself fitting into one of the custody and visitation descriptions below and see which one fits you the best. Everyone knows and understands that your desire to be around the children all the time is as much for their benefit as it is for yours. The whole point of this, however, is to get you to realistically consider where your life is going to be six months after the judge issues his or her judgment.

TYPICAL OR ORDINARY

The most common and usual type of time sharing is the one that you're probably most familiar with. This involves the children living with one parent the majority of the time. The secondary or visiting parent would typically have the kids every other weekend, alternating holidays, and splitting major holidays like Christmas, summers, and, in some cases, spring break. There can be, but may not always include, an evening for dinner and possibly overnight during the course of the week. You'll have to check your local rules to find out if there is an administrative order in your jurisdiction that specifies what usual or common visitation is made up of. There can be pretty specific exceptions to the rule that I've just laid out for you.

The visiting parent will generally be responsible for picking the kids up from school on Friday night before the weekend visit. The same visiting parent is generally responsible for taking the kids back on Sunday night before the next Monday's school. If there is a Friday holiday or a Monday holiday involved in the visiting parent's scheduled weekend, that Friday or Monday is added on to the weekend visit. My experience is that the Fridays and Mondays off in the school calendar will generally "equal" each other out over the course of the school year.

The major holidays that will be divided or split would be, in the typical Christian community, Christmas, Easter (or spring break), summer, and Thanksgiving. These holidays can be either alternated or divided and sometimes both. The design of the visitation is up to you to negotiate or, as a last resort, for the judge to design for you.

Jewish, Muslim, or other religious holidays, if they are observed by the parties, would have to be identified for the court and there would have to be a special design made to deal with those. If these special holidays are of significant importance to you, you will have to tell the judge and suggest a schedule that will give them to you. In a mixed family, for example, where there may be one Christian parent and one Jewish parent, the judge will have an easier task in giving the Jewish holidays to the person of Jewish descent, and the Christian holidays to the person of Christian descent. All of this can be tailor-made to fit your family.

The Christmas holiday and the summer holiday can either be alternated or split depending on the needs of the parents and the children. Some jurisdictions require these holidays to be split and the judge must be convinced to do otherwise. Some jurisdictions require that they are alternated and the judge will have to be convinced to do otherwise. In some jurisdictions summer with the visiting spouse is can be as little as two weeks or as much as half the summer. It is my experience that the visiting spouse would be able to choose which two weeks or the part of summer he or she will visit with the children with notice being given to the custodial spouse in ample time for everyone to make their plans. "First pick" can be a matter that's negotiated, however.

I told you before that Christmas holiday can be split. This generally means one week with one parent and one week with the other. This can sometimes cause problems if one parent or the other wants to take a vacation with the children over this holiday. Sometimes the split occurs the day after Christmas so that the parent with the first part of the holiday has Christmas day and transfers the children to the other parent the afternoon of Christmas day where they will stay until they go back to school in January. This division can be negotiated or designed by the judge depending upon the needs and the wants of the children and the parents. For example, I practiced for years in central Florida where there is a large population of Spanish and Cuban people. I found out after a very short time in practice that in many Spanish and Cuban families, the night **before** Christmas is as important if not more important than the day of Christmas. They call it "Noche Buena" and it involves a traditional meal, opening presents, and bringing as many generations of the family together as is possible in one place. I discovered that in a typical mixed family, the Cuban or Spanish parent was much more anxious to have as part of their time the night before Christmas as they were to have the actual day of Christmas. If you have these sorts of traditions in your family, you must tell your lawyer so that he or she can design a visitation schedule that accommodates these kinds of family or cultural events.

The Thanksgiving holiday is typically alternated. However, here again, if one parent or the other has a large family in the area and has a specific request for the day of Thanksgiving that can be accommodated by the judge, it will be typically awarded to that parent. If both parents have families in the area, it will probably be alternated.

WORK RELATED VISITATION SCHEDULES

Some parents have work schedules that don't lend themselves to the ordinary type of visitation or just make the ordinary type of visitation impossible. Typically, these are the parents who are in the military, possibly firefighters, and possibly police. Is this is not altogether exclusive list, however. There may be people whose careers have always, or of necessity, involve shiftwork, like hospital physicians, nurses, or other careers like that. A lot of police and firefighters have days on and days off that don't necessarily adhere to Monday through Friday. Their visitation times will often have to be designed to fit their work. If they can adjust their work schedules, the court will make them do it to get weekends off, **but,** if it becomes an impediment to their career or it forces them to change careers, their time with the children will have to be negotiated or specifically designed by the judge.

Military personnel are a different problem, of course. Since we have been at war all around the world for so long, a person who has been on deployment will probably never be able to make up the time missed with his or her children. However, in the eyes of the court, the time will have probably been missed anyway even if they were not divorced or not separating. My experience has been that a person who comes off deployment will probably receive the entire next major holiday as part of the make-up time with the children and then go back to a more normal or ordinary visitation schedule. If the deployments are rapid and recurring, the court will have to design something specific. A deployment out of the country that could include children will either have to be negotiated among the parties or designed specifically by the judge including the cost of transportation.

SPLIT VISITATION OR EQUAL TIME SHARING

Some states and jurisdictions now allow for what has become known as equal time sharing or split visitation. This means that the parties share the children on a 50/50 basis or something closely related to it. There are states and jurisdictions that have in their statutes or administrative rules everything from a preference to split custody, no preference for split custody, or language that may discourage split custody. You're going to have to ask your lawyer and research your local jurisdiction to find out if this is something that is preferred, not preferred, or frowned upon.

Split custody is a difficult thing to arrange and for the most part has to be agreed upon by the parties. The judge will also have to make a finding in most jurisdictions that the split custody arrangement is in the best interest of the children as well. Split custody is so difficult because the time-sharing arrangement either alternates weeks or splits the time in the middle of the week, and the children are constantly moving back and forth between one household in another. There is an exception to this, however. I have seen certain circumstances where the parties agree that maintaining the former family home was so important that the parents would move in and out of the house on a weekly basis and alternate going to a separate residence somewhere else. This, of course, was to try to keep the kids in the family home. That is very rare and unusual and causes all kinds of problems also.

In order for split custody to work at all, the parents usually have to be completely in agreement and on the same page as far as transfer of custody, schools, and virtually everything about the children. Many judges and jurisdictions require the parents to live close enough together that the children can ride their bikes back and forth between the parents' households.

LIMITED AND SUPERVISED VISITATION

There are times and circumstances were visitation with the children is limited by the court or supervised under court order.

The reasons for this are many and varied. The visiting parent may be having trouble with drugs or alcohol and possibly shouldn't be trusted with the children for more than a few hours or days at a time. The visiting parent may be so irresponsible that the court is only comfortable giving him or her custody of the children under the supervision of some third party.

Supervision in these circumstances is rarely by the other parent. The chances of arguments and animosity are just too high. The supervisor generally must be arranged by the visiting parent and if the supervisor is to be paid, the expense will be paid by the visiting parent as well. There can be many reasons for this. Drugs and alcohol are the most common but there can be others. I personally handled a number of cases where a visiting parent was recently released from prison or from some sort of rehabilitation facility or confinement, and the court and the custodial parent felt that there needed to be some limits and some supervision for a period of time before the children could be fully integrated back into the visiting parent's life. Limitations and supervision by statute are not to be used for punishment; however, I have known judges to impose limitations and supervision schemes, at least for a period of time, for just those purposes. I should mention that drinking and driving with the children in the car is something that will cause you to lose custody of the children pretty routinely. If you don't have primary custody of the children but you are visiting, drinking and driving with the children in the car will probably end up limiting your visits or possibly injecting a supervisor into your relationship with the children to make sure that they're safe when they're in your care.

SOLE CUSTODY OR DENIED VISITATION

This is self-explanatory. There are circumstances and facts that can demand or require that visitation be denied to a noncustodial parent. In these situations, the visiting parent will have to earn his or her way back to a situation that they might be trusted with visitation again.

Any judgment that contains a limitation or provision for supervision or denial of visitation has to be accompanied by a written opinion by the judge that the limitation, supervision, or denial of visitation is in the best interest of the child or children. The opinion also usually contains specific reasons why the judge feels that the limitations on restrictions are necessary. The reasoning behind this is obvious. Taking away a parent's right to even see his or her children is an extreme step. Both the custodial parent and the parent who loses visitation rights are entitled to have a specific record detailing the action and the reasons for the action. The custodial parent needs it for future hearings or court cases when the judge who originally issued the order is not available or possibly retired. The parent who lost the right to visit needs the detailed order for a time in the future when he or she tries to change the denial or restrictions. If the reasons for the drastic actions are not there anymore and he or she is capable of resuming contact with the kids, that person needs a description of what the problem was in order to describe the steps that have been taken to correct them.

3

How's It Going to Get Started?

WHO WILL IT BE?

Someone has to file a petition for divorce containing a custody and/or a visitation complaint, a paternity action, or just a custody and visitation action under the UCCJEA. Who is that somebody? It can be by married people with a child or children, a couple who has never been married but the paternity of the child has been determined already, a parent who has been living with a child and wants to establish paternity (who's the father?), or even a man who believes he's the father of a child and hasn't been recognized by the law (or the Mom) as the father. You do NOT have to be married to start a custody action. You simply must have a well-founded belief that you're a parent.

There are exceptions to these rules. The first is easy. A parent or parents who adopt a child are, in the eyes of the law, the parents even though there is no blood relationship, so they can be parties to a custody and/or visitation case.

The next is interesting. I personally represented a mother in the following circumstances. She was pregnant for two months. The biological father was not in the picture anymore. She met a new man and they fell in love. They married before the baby's birth. The husband, even knowing he was not the child's biological father, signed and acknowledged that he was the father of the child in the hospital. They lived together for another few years. During that time the husband took the child as a deduction on his taxes, insured the child on his health insurance as his own, and held the child out to the world as his child. In the divorce proceeding, he denied the child was his. The judge said that he made the child his by his actions, not only on the birth certificate but in the time after that, too. The purpose of the law is not to make children illegitimate. The thought is that having claimed the child and having accepted the benefits of paternity, neither the mother nor the father in that situation could then refuse to be a parent (with all of the responsibilities) after that. The troublesome idea that comes to mind at this point is what about the husband who thought all along he was the father but was not? Adultery is a universal ground for divorce in states that utilize "grounds" as a requisite for divorce. After many years, does the birth of an illegitimate baby overcome the presumption that the husband is the father? In some, if not most, states, the answer is yes, but you'll have to ask your lawyer about yours.

The last exception is different among the states and you will have to consult with your attorney about this. The UCCJEA speaks about parents having the ability to make claims for custody and sometimes "those in the place of or acting as parents." Think about it. That may mean that grandparents, aunts, uncles, or others acting as parents may have "standing" or the ability to make a claim for custody or visitation. The reason I said you'll have to talk to a lawyer about it is because the rules and conditions under which a grand parent, etc., can make such a claim are as different and varied as the number of states we have. Some states say grandparents acting as parents can be parties to custody cases. Some states say "no way."

ON SURROGATE MOMS
AND SPERM DONOR DADS

The rules are being set right now. The cases are still rare dealing with the rights of people in this position. For the most part they're not set in stone and are still being decided on the "best interest of the child" test. That means there are no rules. These cases are passing through courts as I write and you read this, and I suspect we'll see legislation on it soon. You'll have to ask your lawyer about it if you find yourself in this position. I think that the sooner we do set rules for the parents who desperately want kids and the surrogate moms and donor dads who want relationships with these kids the better off we'll be. Some states are working with it and some aren't. I will tell you this. The Kansas court has just allowed the Kansas Department of Children and Families to sue a sperm donor for child support in a case where a same sex couple broke up and the non-custodial parent did not adopt the child. There was an agreement by all parties that the sperm donor would NEVER be asked to be responsible or participate in the raising or support of the child. It seems to leave the way open for the sperm donor, at least in Kansas, to seek custody or visitation if he's responsible for support.

HOW DOES IT START?

The technical way this gets started is like any other lawsuit. That is with a summons and petition. I described in *Divorce and Conquer* most of that process, but there are some special aspects to any custody and visitation action.

First is something we've already talked about. There must be a UCCJEA affidavit filed with the petition. With no affidavit, there is no chance of getting custody or visitation. It's jurisdictional, which means it has to be there. Some lawyers include the affidavit right in the original petition. Some set it out as a separate paper attached to the petition. Some rules require it to be separate, some don't. This is a technical aspect that you'll have to find out or rely on your lawyer to give you.

There must be a paragraph in the petition that makes a claim for custody or visitation or both. The claim must be followed by a request in the "prayers" section of the lawsuit (which describes to the judge what you want), a request that you be given custody, visitation or both.

The petition is hand served on the other parent or it can be received by your or your spouse's lawyer by agreement. The general rules of pleadings apply. That means the paragraphs in the petition must be clear enough to give the other party a clear, detailed understanding of what you're saying and what you want. This is a place to be **VERY CAREFUL**. Most jurisdictions and every judge I've ever known frown upon, if not prohibit, parties from telling the kids what's in the petition other than it's about custody and visitation. It seems like sooner or later, however, one or the other will tell or show them anyway. That is the reason for the care in what goes in the petition. If you say too little, the kids will think you don't want them or worse you're failing to protect them. If you say too much, they may think you're exposing too much about them or, worse than that, lying. You have to say enough to get the point across but not enough to embellish or lie. A lie can cause all kinds of problems and not just with the kids. Your spouse will hold it against you and NEVER negotiate with you about anything again. A lie discovered by your lawyer may be grounds for him to quit and to maybe keep all of the money you gave him. A lie discovered by the judge will make you a liar in his or her eyes from that minute forward and could lose the kids for you. A lie that a lawyer talks you into making for purposes of flashy pleadings is a breach of ethics for him or her, but they'll blame it on you. If it's discovered by the judge, all of the above bad things will happen. The judge will believe the lawyer and you'll be proven a liar. Your spouse will never believe you or negotiate with you again. (And why should they?) You'll probably lose the case because the judge doesn't believe you anymore. I told you in *Divorce and Conquer* to stay away from a lawyer who tells you it is okay to lie anywhere. This is the most important part of that warning.

If you are the petitioner, then you've already filled out the documents I'm going to talk about now. If you are the respondent or the defendant as sometimes you'll be known, you will have to talk to your lawyer and design an answer and probably a counter petition.

If you are the respondent or defendant (as they are sometimes known) the *answer* is your first document to be filed. It will respond item by item to the paragraphs in the petition. Generally these responses will be either admitted or denied. Sometimes there may be a request for further clarification of the paragraph, but for the most part you will simply admit or deny the allegations (what your spouse or co-parent says in his or her petition). You will probably then find a section that is called the prayers in your answer where your lawyer will ask the court to deny or dismiss everything that your spouse has said about you, the children, as well as their prayers for relief. Prayers for relief are the paragraphs generally found at the bottom of the petition which ask the judge to do something.

Most of the time your lawyer will also dictate a counter petition. Your counter petition contains paragraphs that make statements about yourself, your spouse, and the children setting up the case for giving you custody or visitation in some form. This is where I warned you to be careful in their earlier pages. Your counter petition will also include a prayers section in which you will make specific requests for action by the judge in giving you custody or visitation, sometimes both. The answer and counter petition is most often signed by you, although it can be signed by your lawyer and your lawyer can file an affidavit on your behalf agreeing to everything said in the counter petition and the answer.

In most jurisdictions the rules require you to file a financial affidavit either immediately with the petition or the answer and counter petition or very shortly thereafter. The reason for this is that in most cases, custody and visitation will have a request or prayer for financial relief in the form of child support and possibly attorney's fees. Child support or attorney's fees are subjects that I'll take up in another place but most rules require a financial affidavit to be filed with or shortly after the filing of the petition or answer and counter petition.

So, what you'll be doing immediately is filing in the same court where the petition was filed, your answer, counter petition, financial affidavit, and your UCCJEA affidavit. In some circumstances your lawyer will also follow immediately with discovery requests which we took up in the first volume.

Your answer to the petition must be filed within 20 days of your receipt of the petition in every jurisdiction I've ever heard of. If your answer is not filed within the 20 days (in some cases extended by five days to allow for mailing) you may be subject to default. A request for default is a document filed when one party does not file a required response within the time allotted by the rules. The default can mean a number of things. The worst of these is that the judge grants your spouse's requests because you have not denied them. It's never a good idea to allow your response to go into a state of default even for a day or two. It is possible to get a default overturned, but generally it is required that you and/or your attorney prove to the court that the lateness of your response was caused by excusable neglect or other circumstances that can be excused by the court, such as illness, unavailability of your lawyer, or something like that. The best thing that you can do is to at all times avoid a default so that you never have to ask a judge to set it aside.

These are the steps that will be taken at the beginning of the custody and visitation lawsuit. There may be other items included in the petition. If you want a divorce, the lawyer will ask for a divorce in the original petition. If you want alimony, property division, possibly exclusive use and possession of a piece of real estate or personal property like a car, child support or attorney's fees, all of these things will be covered in paragraphs in the petition and the counter petition. To leave these items out most probably will preclude you from getting them from the judge in the future. I told you before that the general rules of pleading apply.

That means you must draft paragraphs for each one of the items that you want, like the ones mentioned above, and if you do not, you can't get them. Be careful to go over each and every one of the items you want with your lawyer before you sign your petition, answer, or counter petition.

I don't want to get into this too deeply, but you may only be able to ask for the things like alimony and/or property division in a case for divorce. Some states don't give unmarried people the right to ask for them.

4

How Do We Prepare the Case for Custody and/or Visitation?

FIRST MAKE SOME DECISIONS

Many jurisdictions and most (probably yours) have rules and lists of matters that a judge may and should consider in making a determination of what has previously been known as custody. You have noticed that I've used that word "custody" because it is widely accepted outside of the legal community as descriptive of what we are doing. I'm going to try to interpret the legalese now so that you will understand the current state of the law and the language that you will hear in your lawyer's office when you talk about the subject.

SHARED PARENTAL RESPONSIBILITY

Shared parental responsibility is a "legal fiction." To describe what I mean by legal fiction it's easier to talk about real property. In the situation of a husband and wife, the ownership of a house grants upon them and each of them full ownership of the house. This means that each of them own one hundred percent of the entire legal description. Obviously, it's difficult for two people to own one hundred percent of anything, especially when they're not friends anymore. They have conflicting interests, and if they divorce, their actual percentage of ownership will have to be decided by a judge or, in some cases, a jury. This is the same concept as Shared Parental Responsibility. Both parents and spouses have full responsibility and rights for and over the children. When parties divorce or when a family breaks up, the different areas of responsibility, as well as the percentages of time spent with each parent, have to be decided. Obviously, as in the case of the real estate, the two parents, now separated, cannot have one hundred percent of the time with the children. But they do still retain one hundred percent responsibility for and over the children. Divorcing and/or separating parents who are awarded shared parental responsibility still maintain their rights to make decisions for and that affect the children. Decisions such as whether the child gets braces, goes to private school, or any other life track decisions still remain in joint hands. These decisions or areas of control can be divided up by the judge or in some cases by the parents by agreement. If the parents cannot agree on things like braces or private school, then one or the other of the parents may be given that responsibility. In the worst-case scenario, the parties may have to go back to court to get an order from the judge for decisions like this.

PRIMARY AND SECONDARY RESIDENTIAL CARE

Primary residential care is defined very simply as the parent who has the majority of the time with the child and the person who is first on the contact list on school records, doctor records, and a few other places. Secondary residential care refers to the other parent. However, the secondary residential parent is listed immediately below the primary in those records. In some extreme cases, the primary parent may be granted larger or more sweeping rights and powers, but those will only be when a judge thinks it's appropriate. These two designations are the most often and hotly contested of any actions within the major heading of divorce and child custody. It is generally the primary residential custodian whose address is listed on school and doctor records, etc. It is generally the primary residential custodian who is referred to as the primary caretaker on school or medical documents as well. However, the primary residential custodian has the responsibility and duty to make sure that any information passed from the school, or the doctor, or the counselor gets to the secondary residential custodian on an immediate if not very quick basis. In most cases it is the duty of the primary residential caretaker to see to it that the providers like the doctor and the school have the name address and phone number for the secondary residential caretaker. The subject of whether or not you should contest these designations is something you should think about for a long time and discuss thoroughly with your lawyer before you undertake the fight.

There is still a feeling in most women's minds that they should always be designated primary residential caretaker. It is felt that if they do not receive this designation that they are somehow less than they should be or that friends and relatives will consider them less than they should be. So many women now have full-time careers that it is impossible for those women to even consider being primary residential caretakers. This is not to say that a woman who is not employed or employed in the home is not still the optimum choice for the children and the most obvious for the judge. Understand, however, that if the situation is reversed and it is the husband or male parent who is more available to the children on a regular and routine basis, he may be the one more desirable for the job.

Something that is almost always forgotten in the consideration of whether to make a fight out of custody and visitation is the "post dissolution (divorce) environment." Parties should remember that they will be single after this is over. What that means is you will **not** have the day-to-day participation and help of your spouse or other parent to rely on. If you have an emergency that arises on your job and you have not made arrangements for the children after school, you may be in real trouble if your ex-spouse can't be available. If you have been through a protracted and angry custody fight, you can depend on the LACK of cooperation that you'll receive from that person. If the custody action has been agreeable and you have been able to negotiate times, places, and exchanges with your other parent, you may be able to call that person to help out at any time.

The other thing that has to be remembered is that being single means a totally new social environment and in many cases a totally new set of friends. Generally people who go through a custody and visitation fight are young enough (since the kids are under 18) that they will want to reestablish a social life and may even want to date and try again. Remember, this takes time. If you have fought for and won a custody fight, your ex spouse is not going to be so happy hear from you at all, let alone if you're asking for him or her to take the kids out of turn so you can go out on a date. Your new circle of friends (and probably some of the old ones now that you're single) will want to get you out and doing things that possibly you haven't done for a while. If you don't have a good working relationship with your ex, you will be limited and restricted to only the times that the kids are with him or her. The only other alternative is to hire a baby-sitter which will usually have to be "vetted" by your ex, and will be a huge expense to you.

I'm sure that what you've all ready determined is that I am trying to convince you to negotiate whenever possible with regard to custody, visitation, and exchange times. Historically, if you can negotiate with your ex during the course of the lawsuit, you can be negotiable with your ex after it's over (and they will be negotiable with you). Also you can probably tell I am trying to make you aware that fighting for every possible minute of the children's time probably is not only not fair to your ex, it will sooner or later not be fair to you. There will come a time that the children will also be telling you when they're going to see their other parent, and the older they get the less control you have over this. Is it smart to have a protracted, angry, and VERY expensive fight for a visitation schedule that may last for only a year or two?

I have mentioned exchange times and places before. You may not think this is such a huge issue but it becomes one at some point in time between exes. You should also be negotiable on this issue as well because sooner or later you or the other parent will want to change it or move it because of some unforeseen circumstance.

Having your new friend (when that happens) drop off the kids at your ex's house is not a great idea for a while either. It only draws the new friend into the argument.

LET'S GET STARTED

WHAT WE DO FIRST?

My first suggestion is to begin reading. Get all of the books and articles you can on shared parental responsibility, dealing with an ex-spouse or co-parent, children of divorce, or any other reading material that you can to help you navigate your way through the new reality. You should keep a list or bibliography of this material. The judge will want to know what effort or steps you have taken to prepare yourself for being a part-time parent and dealing with another part-time parent. It can't hurt and it may just impress the judge.

Ask your lawyer about any required courses in shared parental responsibility that may be part of the process you must undertake in order to get a judgment. In many jurisdictions the rules require that parents take the course just to continue on with the lawsuit. You may as well get started on it early and you will be able to tell the court (judge) when he asks you or tells you to take it that you all ready have. If there's more than one course, take a couple. As I said before, it can't hurt and it may impress the judge. You will at the very least meet other people who are going through the same trauma and maybe they have some ideas you haven't thought of.

Get in the habit of taking notes. Keep a notepad or pocket dictator with you all the time. You may be thinking that this is to write down all the bad things your ex is doing, but you're wrong. You need to start thinking about the list the judge will be thinking about. There is a list that every judge is supposed to use to evaluate in making a custody and visitation order which we're about to get into in the next chapter. If you can make lists and notes for yourself, it will be of huge benefit to your lawyer when he or she starts going through the list for the judge in court on trial day(s).

Use e-mail and handwritten notes (that you always copy) when you contact your ex. There are a few reasons for this. First, you want to show yourself to be the parent who "includes" the other parent on *everything*. If "Johnnie" fell down but didn't require a doctor, shoot off an email so your ex knows about it. If he got an A on a quiz in class, shoot off an email. If you do this, the ex can never say you don't keep him or her informed, and it shows both your ex and the judge you're making sure they know everything. However, never pass a note or message using your child as the courier. It gets the child too involved in parental communication and can lead to some bad results.

Don't ever argue or raise your voice with your ex in the presence of your child. I know this will be a tough one because most of your contact after separation will be at "pick-up and drop-off points" so it will be the time you'll be most tempted to get into it with them. You must never be the one who shouts because the children, your neighbors, and anyone else around (witnesses) will remember your tone and your words. Most often these are the words you'll regret but everyone else will remember. An argument or disagreement should be done outside the hearing of the children. If it becomes abusive or your spouse insists on having it in front of the kids, stop and contact your lawyer during the next available business hours. Calls to a lawyer at night or over the weekend are never welcome and always expensive. I routinely charged $500 for weekend calls.

5

The Things a Judge Will Want Proof Of

This is the section that will be the longest and most important.

Most states (there's that phrase again) will have in their custody and visitation statutes or laws a list of items that the legislature in that state has decided should be the basis on which they want their judge or judges to decide custody and visitation. The statutes themselves will specify these items as factors affecting the welfare and interests of the particular minor child or children for purposes of establishing or modifying, creating, developing, or approving time-sharing schedules and the existence and duration of visitation matters.

Some states put more emphasis on some items rather than others, and you will have to consult with your attorney on which are the most important versus which are secondary. You should not be discouraged if your evaluation on each one of these items results in a "draw" between you and your ex. There probably will be many situations where you and your ex are equal, or there is no clear winner. In that case it may be up to the judge to evaluate the rest of the factors to make a determination. In all circumstances, the best interest of the child or children is mandated to be the highest consideration even over all of the rest of the factors. Each of these factors may be different or contain slightly different language. The statute will very probably contain these factors in some form or another. Some states may have some of the factors and some may have others. You may even find that your state has combined two or more of them into one.

THIS IS IMPORTANT. I'm going to get into your parenting plan and the factors to be shown to the judge as to why you should be chosen to have the kids, or why you should have extended visits with the children. Preparation is EVERYTHING. You should write down the responses to these factors and present them to your lawyer. That's why I suggested you carry a note pad or pocket dictator during this ordeal. You'll probably want to change slightly or modify your responses on these factors. They should be presented to the judge with your parenting plan. I would never call a judge lazy or forgetful, but I have had the experience that a judge may misplace or not fully appreciate evidence that is presented to him or her. If you present the responses to these factors in a neat, organized form and the parenting plan is a fully explained, coherent form IN WRITING, even a judge who has heard twenty cases in a week will remember your points. As a matter of fact, if you present these to the judge but your ex does not, it may be the only concrete material the judge has to base his or her ruling on. Make sure these writings are in the trial file before the case is finished. Work with the lawyer's para-legal or legal assistant to make sure they're done.

Remember this list is **not** exclusive and there can be other things in your state that your statute or rules say are extremely important. You must talk to your lawyer about any peculiar or additional matters you should be thinking about presenting to the judge as part of your proof and to justify your parenting plan.

Your parenting plan is the outline for your relationship, your ex's relationship, and your kid's relationship to each other. You should start thinking about it immediately after the first meeting with your lawyer. The parenting plan will include:

1. The placement of the kids with regard to primary and secondary residential care.

2. A schedule that is as accurate as you can make it proposing the times and, if possible, the dates and even places of the transfer of physical custody of the kids including who is responsible for transportation of the kids on those dates and at those times.

3. Any designation or assignment of responsibilities regarding issues like taking the kids to the doctor, to extracurricular activities, tutoring, or any other responsibility you may find necessary to put into writing.

4. If necessary, your parenting plan should have specific provisions for communication between the two of you in the accepted methods and times for the said communication. If necessary, you may want to specify a particular phone number or address for communication. You also may want to stipulate a specific phone number for the kids to call when they're not in your presence. I've had some luck

with the kids actually having their own cell phone for the purpose of making calls while on visitation or while in the custody of the other spouse. This may be a phone that the other parent is specifically prohibited from taking away from the children unless by agreement. In really difficult cases, some parents have to schedule telephone calls daily or weekly to the noncustodial spouse so that time schedules and activities don't interfere.

5. Any other provisions that are necessary to describe the relationship as you see it after the entry of the final judgment of custody and visitation.

You may want to consider the kids' relationships with their grandparents, step-siblings, or any other third party relationships that are in the kids' lives now that you want to continue as part of the parenting plan so that if the relationship between you and your ex becomes so strained that you can't negotiate anymore, at least you'll have some of these issues specified.

You can't consider all contingencies. It's just impossible. You should, however, make notes and think about what happens during the course of the legal proceedings. These are the sorts of things that will come back later. You can design a cure or a "fix" for these matters in the parenting plan if you work on it. Some parts of the parenting plan can be negotiated and it may be that some parts can't. Try to get the ones that can be worked out between you and your ex reduced to writing before you even go to court so that they don't change their mind and try to bring those issues up later. Be as through as possible.

Let's start.

1. The demonstrated capacity and disposition of

each parent to facilitate and encourage a close and continuing parent–child relationship, to honor the time-sharing schedule and to be reasonable when changes are required.

This is the most important in some states and some courts. You must present yourself and present evidence to the judge that you are the choice of the two parents that will at all times encourage a relationship with your ex. I know at this moment in time that seems counterintuitive and NOT what you want to do. You're trying to convince the judge to give you the kids most of the time however, to do that, you have to prove you're the one who will give the co-parent the most time after the order is written. Whether you mean it or whether you don't, you're going to have to convince the judge through witnesses and evidence that you will encourage the relationship of the kids with your ex. Additionally, this factor is the one that requires you to always honor the spirit as well as the letter of the time-sharing agreement that is either ordered by the court or agreed upon by the two of you.

I told you earlier that you should begin writing notes and e-mails. This is one of the places where it can be of huge benefit. For example, after your separation but before your trial, there may be a time that your ex asks you to trade times with him or her. Unless you have some event that has been planned for months and already paid for that you absolutely can't cancel, you should trade times. It may be difficult to do it over and over and you may have to bite your tongue but unless there is some real overriding reason, you should go ahead and trade. If there comes a time that you must trade or need to swap with your ex, you should ask but not insist. Just do it by e-mail or by written note and be sure to get a note or an e-mail back. Remember, if your spouse unreasonably refuses, this is evidence against him or her.

Under this factor, you are also required to encourage the child or children to speak or visit with the other parent. There may have been and in many cases will be a moment when your child or children do not want to leave your house or custody or they do not want to go back to your ex's custody. This will probably be one of the most difficult moments in your pretrial experience. You must encourage the child to go back. You must encourage sometimes in forceful terms the child to go on the scheduled visitation even though the child is reluctant. You may even have to tell the child that they have a responsibility to continue their relationship with your ex even though you have a significant problem with it personally. You may even want to tell your ex about the trouble you're having with the child. You could ask if there could be anything you could do to help convince the child to go.

If there is some issue of abuse, either physical or mental, you should bring the question of the abuse to the attention of your lawyer so that he or she can bring it to the attention of the judge. Be careful about this, however, as it may be seen as an attempt to poison the judge or the children against your ex. Abuse is something that has to be proven and, in most cases conclusively, before judge will act on it. There is a section later on spousal abuse and child abuse, but I have to bring it up here because there's always a question.

This factor can be of utmost importance. The children should not be making decisions on when they go and when they don't. You don't let them decide their own bed times or whether they eat their vegetables, do you? Right, then they shouldn't be deciding when they see their other parent. If this is really a problem, you may want to bring it up in one of the other factors, like the "love and affection" section or the "child's preference" section.

2. The anticipated division of parental responsibilities after the litigation including the extent to which parental responsibilities will be delegated to third parties.

In many states, your parenting plan presented to the judge is required to have a section on a division of parental responsibilities after the conclusion of your divorce or custody case. A lot of care needs to go into this before it reaches its final form. You will want to have a fully "fleshed out" and written plan to present to the judge at your trial.

THIS IS IMPORTANT. The parenting plan is something that you should be working on and refining throughout the trial preparation period. This is not something you wait to do. It should be a work in progress from the first day and only be concluded just before the trial. It should be written and suitable to give to the judge as part of your case.

I have seen parenting plans that are extremely loose and unstructured. This usually occurs when the parties are of the same mind and in basic agreement on almost, if not all, issues. It is rare, however, that exes can get to this point. For the most part, most parenting plans contain paragraphs that deal with specific areas of influence and control. For example, if you have been the parent who routinely deals with your child or children's medical issues, it should be specific in your parenting plan that you will continue in that capacity. However, if it has been the custom in your house prior to separation that your ex was the one who dealt with scholastic or school issues and the teachers, then your ex should be the one who probably deals with those in the future. These are pretty general designations but they may be necessary in the post-dissolution (divorce) environment. The vast majority of former spouses or exes, in my experience, have trouble agreeing on much of anything. You must be the one to put away your anger or sense of betrayal and learn to deal with your ex solely on the basis of his or her role as parent.

Parental responsibilities that are designated to third parties can be troublesome. It may be that your parents or your ex's parents have agreed to pay for and supervise your children's education. If you and your ex can agree on it, this may be a situation where a third-party could be designated to have some limited parental responsibility. I'm not a big fan of this kind of thing, however. Your parents will always be looking out for you, and your ex's parents will always be looking out for your ex. Think it over.

There may be a parental responsibility designation left to a third party in the form of a trustee or caretaker of funds possibly. For example if your child has or owns property or wealth on their own but neither of you can agree on how to operate it or control it, there may be a situation that you could designate some third-party in that situation. Again, I'm not a big fan of this unless the property or money is really large and the operation and maintenance may expose you to some kind of legal liability either to the child or your ex. In this limited situation, it may be good to have a trustee to handle this fund or property.

3. The love and affection, bonding, and emotional ties existing between each parent and the child.

In some states this is the biggest factor. It should be a big factor in your determination and decision as well. It is not unusual for this factor to be a draw between parents. If you hope to count this factor in your column, you will be required to show that, for whatever reason, there is a greater bonding of the child to you than to your ex. The classic situation, of course, is the absentee parent. If your ex travels significantly, is or has been gone for a significant period of time, or has over the course of years worked at night when the child was asleep and was asleep when the child was awake, this may be a situation that this factor would be clear for the judge. In most cases, however, given equal daytime jobs, this is going to be a tough one to prove. Even in the case of soldiers or firefighters or when the job requires the parent to be gone for days or weeks, the courts are reluctant to make a determination based on just the job requirement. In order for this to be a winner in those situations, there'll have to be more. In those cases, the soldier or the firefighter will have to express an intent to continue deployments, or continue to be gone from the family for extended periods of time in order for a judge to find that job to be a convincing factor. You should be aware, that if you are married to a soldier or a firefighter, or someone whose job requires frequent or prolonged absences, judges will do everything in their power to make the children available when that person is not deployed and not on a two or three day shift. What that means is that the judge may say that you have primary residential care, but your soldier or firefighter spouse will have the kids whenever he or she is not working.

This item is usually determined by history as I said earlier. If you have been a stay-at-home mom or dad, your child or children are probably more emotionally tied to you. If your spouse is the one who comes home from work, however, and is involved in athletics every afternoon or the children's homework every afternoon, your spouse may be the one the children may be more emotionally tied to.

A word of warning here. In almost every relationship, there is a stronger and a weaker partner. Children, in my experience, naturally gravitate to the weaker of the two. They can in some circumstances become the caretaker, at least in their minds, of the weaker parent. Children can express a great emotional tie to a parent who is addicted to alcohol or emotionally unstable. It is not unusual that a child will want to protect this parent and will express a desire to be with him or her a great deal of the time in order to provide that protection and care. If you think this situation may apply to your family dynamic, it is important that you bring this out to your lawyer so that he or she can arrange for a custody evaluation. The custody evaluation will bring out this problem and the evaluator in most circumstances will be able to deal with it either in the report or by recommendation to the judge as far as a final determination of custody and visitation.

If there is an issue of a child having a trust issue with a parent, or abuse of any kind, this is a place to get the child to a custody evaluator also.

4. The demonstrated capacity and disposition of each parent to determine, consider, and act upon the needs of the child as opposed to the needs or desires of the parents.

This element is not necessarily what you may think when you first read it. Under this criterion the judge will have to make a decision as to which of the two parents will be most likely to act on the needs of the child even if it makes the child unhappy or it makes the child reluctant to spend time with the parent. In order to be the more attractive parent under this factor, you really have to be willing to not only discover but also act on those needs. For example, if the child really requires tutoring in some subject, the parent must be prepared to overcome the reluctant child to make sure that the child has adequate instruction and help.

The part of this factor that differentiates between the needs of the child and the desires of the parents can sometimes be a pretty tough line to walk and requires real strength. The natural desire of a parent is to be friends with a child and have the child really want to be with him or her. In many cases this is something that contesting parents really can't get over. The child may be resistive also and think that for some reason the parent who forces the issue of tutoring or other academic assistance is somehow punishing the child.

I cannot stress strongly enough, however, that even over the child's protests, the judge will be able to see the benefit of granting extended times with the parent who initiates and follows up on things like this. This is one of the tough ones but the importance of it will not be lost on the judge. The tough part is convincing your kid, but isn't that part of your job description as a parent anyway?

The parent who wants to be popular with the children will always come to court and claim the child needs a car or motorcycle when they are the parent who can afford it and they note that their spouse can't. This is a pretty transparent play to get the kids to lean toward moving into the house where the car or motorcycle is available. Judges are pretty perceptive. They'll see it.

In some jurisdictions this factor is simply described as "each parent's knowledge and familiarity of the child in the child's needs." This is a place where you'll want to make sure you know the names and addresses of the child's doctor, school counselor, best friends, and any other pertinent data and information about your child. Even if you have to write them down and keep them in your wallet, these are things that you will want to know on trial day. I can't stress this point on how strong that evidence is. If you're the one who can "rattle off" the doctor's name and the kid's best friends when your spouse can't, it's pretty moving testimony. Likewise, if you're the one who actually takes the child to the doctor or gets the haircuts or goes to baseball practice, it's also pretty strong evidence.

5. The length of time the child has lived in a stable, satisfactory environment and the desirability of maintaining continuity.

There are number of different elements contained within this section. They are all sort of interdependent.

It's the obvious that if a child has lived in a stable satisfactory environment that it would be desirable to maintain the continuity of that environment. Remember that just the length of time is not what this section is about. It is the length of time in a *stable and satisfactory* environment that's the key.

Lots of people and too many lawyers will try to say that just because a child has lived in a place for a long time is a good reason to leave the child there. In actuality, the length of time is just one element. Proving or disproving that the time has been spent in a satisfactory environment is what the judge wants to hear. Spending lots of time in an unstable environment or one that is not satisfactory is a problem.

Let's examine what we're talking about. The stability of the environment can be gauged, for example, by the number of people living in the home, problems in the neighborhood, possibly a problem paying the rent or mortgage or other factors. The child may have lived in a home for a long time but it may not be satisfactory when looked at objectively. We're not talking about just the physical aspects of the home now, although they may be important. The satisfactory qualities of the home may also include problems in the neighborhood as well. My experience is that teenagers need their own rooms. Two or three children of teenage years occupying the same room may not be satisfactory in anyone's eyes, no matter how long they live that way.

In the current economic environment, it's not terribly unusual for different generations of the same family to live in one home. This may or may not be construed as a stable and satisfactory environment, particularly if there is some problem or emotional issue with one or more of the people living in the home. It may not be a good idea to have a teenage girl living in a home with an uncle who drinks too much or has had a problem with drugs. These are the sorts of evaluations that you and your lawyer going to have to make when you're evaluating this criteria.

There is a theory that is popular among psychologists and psychiatrists and others known as "object constancy" and sometimes "attachment theory." The basics of it are that a child will be more comfortable and more secure if they are around and among their own personal items. The child's room, clothes, furniture, toys, and other physical items may be the child's accustomed environment and the professionals seem to think this helps the child with a sense of security after the parents break up. This, of course, seems to give the "home-field advantage" to the parent who is staying in the historical home place after the separation. The professionals are unsure and frankly unclear as to what point in the child's upbringing the object constancy/security issue can be discounted. I have argued and others have as well that the child's bedroom can be duplicated in any house. A child's clothing, pictures, toys, and almost all other personal items can be duplicated or brought to a new home if necessary. If you're willing to do that, you may be able to defeat the object constancy argument. About the only thing that you can't defeat in this situation would be the loss of the child's school and neighborhood friends. But if you're willing to drive to keep the child in school and allow the child to play in the old neighborhood, you may still defeat the argument.

Remember, stable and satisfactory is what the judge is looking for. You may be able to create that stability and satisfactory place in the *future* history. You may be able to make a case that getting the child out of the historical home may **create** the stable environment required by this factor. A better home, better neighborhood, or anything else that improves the environment may be the way to win this one, or at least level the argument.

6. The geographic viability of the parenting plan, with special attention paid to the needs of school-age children and the amount of time to be spent traveling to effectuate the parenting plan.

This factor does not (or at least should not) create a presumption for or against relocation of either parent with a child, but you really have to be careful how far you intend to move away.

We talked about the parenting plan a little bit but it becomes fairly critical when you start talking about moving a child a significant distance away from the parent who's staying in the home.

Moving, even moving to a much better neighborhood, if it's a long distance away, can be a huge problem for children. Children who are attached to their school, their teacher, and their friends in the neighborhood can be resistive and resentful of a move involving many miles. So, the parenting plan has to have "geographic viability" if an ordinary custody and visitation plan is to be attempted. If your move is going to cut off ties to the old neighborhood and the old school, you're probably going to have to find some other way to sell it or justify it to the judge. A move involving more than forty-five minutes or an hour of travel each way is going to be seen as a problem to a lot of judges for kids who have significant attachments to their neighborhood and school. The object constancy and attachment theories that we talked about also come in here.

If your proposed move is one that's going to take the child more than an hour away, you will probably have to work out some sort of transportation plan so the kids can still see their friends or play on the same baseball team.

Sometimes a divorce or separation can be caused by a new job or new opportunities that take one of the parents out of town. It is a real uphill fight to get the kids to go out of town. Generally, you will have to prove that the new position or environment is of such great benefit to the children that leaving them where they are would cause a significant detriment to them. I'll talk about the specifics of an "out-of-jurisdiction" move more later.

The best example I can give you on this is a woman whom I represented once who had two children. Both she and her husband had blue-collar jobs but she was in college for approximately six years before the separation. While she was in college, she had been taking care of the children during the daytime and going to school and working at night while they were asleep. She had been working as a shift waitress in order to partially support the family and pay for her education. When she graduated from college, she was offered a great job (her field was logistics) but it was in Chicago. Her pay at the restaurant had been approximately $250 a week. Her starting salary in Chicago was $90,000—plus it was an ordinary 9-to-5 job. She would not have been able to get a starting salary of even half that much in the local job market. Her husband, the father of the children, of course resisted the notion that the children would be better off in Chicago. We had to present a parenting plan to the judge that called for the children to spend almost all of their vacation time with the father in order to keep and maintain a relationship with him. The judge ultimately found that the parenting plan we proposed would maintain that relationship and the huge opportunity would be of benefit not only to the mom but also to the children. This is a pretty extreme example. But I recounted it to you because it is the type of extreme evidence you'll have to present in order to win custody action if you're planning on taking the kids out of town.

In most circumstances the evidence required is not going to be as difficult as that. But a well thought out and fleshed out parenting plan is something you're going to have to present to the judge even if you're just moving twenty blocks away.

In some circumstances, where one or the other of the parties is suggesting 50/50 time-sharing with the children, you may have to stay even closer than that. A lot of judges want parents to live extremely close to each other if they are going to award

50/50 time-sharing. I've even seen some circumstances were judges want parents to live close enough that the children can bike between the houses. The problems are obvious. If you're going to have a 50/50 time-sharing arrangement, keeping both new residences close together is almost a necessity.

7. The moral fitness of the parents.

In some situations the decision on this one is pretty simple. If one of the parents has a drinking problem, has an uncontrollable drug problem, or is simply morally unfit for one of a hundred other reasons, the decision for the judge is not a problem.

Under ordinary circumstances, though, both parents are equally fit and generally this is a tie.

You should be extremely careful when seeking to prove that your spouse or the other parent is morally unfit. You should have clear and convincing evidence before you even undertake something like this. In this situation if you try to prove that your former spouse or co-parent is morally unfit and you fail to do so, it is worse than having never tried. You should think back to criterion number one (the demonstrated capacity and disposition of each parent to facilitate and encourage a close and continuing parent – child relationship) and think about how this will affect the judge's decision. If your attempt in this regard is so weak and unprovable, the judge just may go back and decide that maybe you're not the person most likely to facilitate and encourage that relationship with the kids. Unless there is something very clear and undeniable in the relationship that points to poor moral fitness, I generally just let this one be a tie. If you go into anything less than obvious evidence, it can be more harmful to you and your cause than the benefit could have ever been.

8. *The mental and physical health of the parents.*

This is another example of a test that in most situations is pretty simple. If one of the parents is emotionally unstable or just physically unable to deal with the day-to-day requirements of being a parent, it's a different story.

As we talked about in item 7, you would have to have very clear and convincing, if not undeniable, evidence of a shortfall in either the mental or physical health of your spouse or co-parent in order for this to be anything but a tie.

I would suggest to you that making a claim that your spouse is mentally unfit would require some sort of clinical diagnosis in order to be a winner. The fact that your ex talks to herself or does odd things would not be enough in the situation. I have always stayed away from this one also because it's just too much of a risk without clear and convincing evidence. Not only would the evidence require a diagnosis by a physician or psychiatrist but in my estimation, it would also require that the physician or psychiatrist say the condition your ex is suffering from would also affect his or her ability to be a parent.

I've seen testimony in court by physicians and psychiatrists that "high functioning" bipolar parents and even parents bordering on being alcoholics have been allowed to keep or have significant time-sharing with children simply because they have been "high functioning" for many years without a single problem. I say this to you because I want make it clear that you should really think this over before you take a chance on it. If you have allowed this "high functioning" parent to be alone with the kids while you lived together, there had better be some sort of change in them that you will rely on when you say that **now** it's not okay.

I want to give you a strong word of warning here. Any person who drinks or uses drugs and then puts the children in the car and drives around will just about guarantee that they lose a custody hearing. Furthermore, any person who gets a DUI while the children are in the car has probably forfeited any chance they may have at unsupervised visitation. I have never known a judge or an instance that behavior like this has been overlooked by a judge. Your ex will bring in witness after witness and expert after expert to testify that if you will do it once you will do it again. There is no excuse for it in my mind and none in any judge's mind either. Any element of trust left between you and your ex will evaporate as soon as they find out about it, and any hope you may have a beneficial settlement or for that matter even any polite conversation with your ex will have just about evaporated. If you find out your ex has done this and you don't report it to the judge, then you are putting the children in as much danger as your ex is when they drink and drive.

Rehabilitating yourself in the eyes of the judge in the case of the DUI with the kids in the car can take years. Your ex will probably never forget it.

A physical disability can also be a minefield for you. If your spouse or co-parent is functioning as a parent and has been for years, you should not attempt to use a physical disability as a reason why they should not have custody or significant time-sharing with the children. If, on the other hand your co-parent or spouse has to have help in order to perform his or her daily functions or physically help with the kids, you may think about it. It's never going to be a happy circumstance, though, because you will be seen to have been critical of a physically disabled person. The physical disability will have to be so profound that probably your ex and the kids will agree it's a problem.

9. *The reasonable preference of the child, if the court deems the child to be of sufficient intelligence, understanding, and experience to express a preference.*

We spoke above about the natural tendency of children to gravitate towards the weaker of the two parents and the child's natural inclination to protect that parent, and in some circumstances act as caretaker for that parent. This is the factor where you're really going to have to differentiate and explain to the judge the difference between the child's desire and what's good for the child.

Most judges will resist the thought of a child coming to court and testifying about preference. It's usually done through a Guardian ad litem or custody evaluator. If the judge is going to let a child come to court and testify, however, the judge will have to make a determination as to the "sufficient intelligence, understanding, and experience to express a preference" by the child. In some states the beginning point of this determination is whether or not the child can understand the nature and importance of an oath.

In many states there is no specific language in the statute concerning when a child can take an oath. For the most part children starting at age twelve are sophisticated enough to understand what an oath is and how important it is. In some states there is a specific starting point or year (generally twelve) that a child can come to court and testify if necessary. Even then the judge has to make a determination as to the motivation behind the child's testimony and if that motivation is a valid. If it can be proven that a child is coming to court to testify simply because he or she is been promised a car, for example, then that testimony will probably not be followed by the judge. Likewise, if the child is testifying because he or she can stay up longer on weekends or will be allowed to date a certain person whom maybe one parent doesn't like, the judge will probably take that into account in weighing the testimony as well.

Interestingly, some states such as Georgia have a provision that a child of fourteen may have the right to select the custodial parent, although that's not universal. You'll have to discuss with your lawyer whether your state has specific statutes or provisions like this, or possibly others, dealing with the child's testimony or preference. Each individual legislature has to make determinations like that and decide if they'll have unique provisions in their own state.

If the child prefers your ex's house because they get to stay up all night, eat ice cream for every meal, and drink beer, it's pretty easy for a judge to determine that their preference is not a good one. The facts are not usually as strong as that, however, and you'll have to work with more subtle reasons.

10. The demonstrated capacity of each parent to communicate with and keep the other parent informed of issues and activities regarding the minor child, and the willingness of each parent to adopt a unified front on all major issues when dealing with the child.

This is another one of those sections that seems almost counterintuitive when you read it for the first time. The court is going to determine which of you has historically been the parent to keep the other informed. The section goes on to specify information about issues and activities regarding the minor child as well as the willingness to present a united front to the child all major issues.

I understand here and the judge understands here that naturally one of the last things you're going to want to do is communicate on a regular basis with your ex. If you're the one who has chosen to leave the relationship, you may even think it will send the wrong message to your ex if you call him or her all of the time. This is a real test for you and you're going to have to really concentrate and be strong to pass it. There may be times when you really don't want to adopt a unified front on major issues with the child and it may seem like you're giving in on some issues. I suggest that when you were still married or still living with your ex, you had to give up some position sometimes on issues that you weren't terribly happy about. This is just another one of those occasions.

How do you prove to the judge that you're the one who is going to be the best choice in this regard? The answer is to adopt or create a habit of contacting the ex any time there is any kind of major juncture or any kind of news item whatsoever, no matter how small. I told you in the past that you should be sending e-mails or handwritten notes. This is another place where e-mails and handwritten notes will serve to establish the *future* history that the judge will be looking for.

Remember it is the **demonstrated** capacity that the statute calls for and that the judge will be looking for. The demonstrated capacity is going to mean the person who goes out of his or her way to make sure the former spouse or co-parent is kept up to date on everything. You will have trouble presenting evidence to demonstrate you have kept your ex up on all of these events with just your testimony. Believe me, when you get to the trial date, your ex will not remember all of the times you have contacted him or her about these issues. Keep those e-mails.

What the judge will be looking for specifically will be school activities, athletic activities (including practices), doctors' appointments, parent/teacher conferences and the like. I've always advised clients that the best way to handle this is to provide a written calendar with all of these items noted, with times, far enough in advance that the co-parent can make arrangements to attend any of these events that he or she cares to. The calendar idea provides two separate valid pieces of evidence. The first is that you are keeping your ex up to speed on all the events in plenty of time, and the second is that you can make notations on the calendar you keep on which of the events the ex chose to attend and which of the events he or she did not attend. The calendar you send the ex should be an exact copy of the one you keep with the exception of your notes on his or her attendance at all these events.

Some people tend to go overboard on these calendars and the e-mail notations. I've never thought it was terribly interesting or terribly important for an ex to be aware of or the timing of events like haircuts. Some people, however, find them to be very important junctures in a child's life. I would suggest to you that if it's the child's first haircut, you'll want to invite the ex. After that, my advice would be to write an e-mail and ask if he or she really wants to be involved in the rest of them. As I said above, the response to this will not only prove that you're the one giving him or her the opportunity, but also will go to show where his or her priorities are with regard to events in the child's life.

The presentation of a unified front in this section is more trouble. You must be willing to negotiate on issues concerning the child and his or her well-being at all times. You'll need to be forceful when it's necessary (without being threatening) but be willing to give up the position if it's not all that important. Issues involving whether or not to go to private school, whether or not to put braces on the child's teeth, or whether or not your daughter should date the boy with the motorcycle are things that will come up during these conversations. You have to make your position clear, so my advice is always to do it in writing. E-mail or handwritten notes are okay, but just remember at all times that sooner or later a judge may read this and make a determination on your fitness to be the primary parent based on what you said and the ideas you put in these notes. What I'm telling you is if you have strong feelings about it; make sure your ex knows it. Just be careful that it doesn't sound threatening and that you are willing to go to court to explain to the judge what you said and why.

You may be familiar with the term, "parental alienation". The accepted definition is " a social dynamic, generally occurring due to divorce or separation, when a child expresses unjustified hatred or unreasonably strong dislike of one parent, making access by the rejected parent difficult or impossible. These feelings may be influenced by negative comments by the other parent and by the characteristics, such as lack of empathy and warmth, of the rejected parent. The term does not apply in cases of actual child abuse, when the child rejects the abusing parent to protect themselves. Parental alienation is controversial in legal and mental health professions, both generally and in specific situations. Terms related to parental alienation include child alienation, pathological alignments, visitation refusal, brainwashing, and pathological alienation." It translates into one parent attempting to poison the mind or minds of the children against the other. It happens occasionally and most, if not all judges find it despicable. It will be found to be a *game changer* if it shows up in your custody litigation. Volumes have been written on the subject and if you suspect it has entered your dynamic, you should tell your attorney or child custody evaluator immediately.

11. Evidence of domestic violence, sexual violence, child abuse, child abandonment, or child neglect, regardless of whether a prior or pending action relating to those issues has been brought.

Generally, if the court accepts evidence of prior or pending actions regarding domestic violence, sexual violence, child abuse, child abandonment, or child neglect, the court must specifically acknowledge in writing that such evidence was considered when evaluating the best interest of the child. In some states it is mandatory that the judge reference the fact that he or she is accepting the evidence and it must be reflected on any judgment awarding or denying custody or visitation.

I warned you before about bringing up domestic violence without proof or without clear evidence to back up your claim. I'm going to do it again because this can be a real minefield without witnesses, x-rays, or photographs to prove it. Men and women are just as guilty of this.

Domestic violence is a truly serious matter, however. Most medium and large circuits or districts have dedicated courts that do nothing but decide criminal domestic violence cases and/or temporary restraining orders regarding domestic violence. So if you have brought a domestic violence action against your ex, either civil or criminal, and you have already won in court, you can make that evidence part of your custody and visitation matter. You just have to go to the court clerk and get certified copies of the judgment. Likewise, if your spouse has brought a criminal or civil action against you for domestic violence and they lost or you were found not guilty, you can bring that into court as part of your evidence. Just be careful.

Sexual violence among spouses is one of the most difficult things to prove in court. Technically, a person can begin an episode of consensual sex and then withdraw the consent after it has begun. Proving that is almost impossible unless there are witnesses who actually see and hear the refusal or resistance. Be very careful on this one as well. That is not to say that there may not be issues of sexual violence among married people. What I am saying is that in order to prove it, you may have to make an outcry to the police and exhibit to them some evidence of resistance before the police will believe you and before judge will believe you.

This section, in my mind, also includes sexual violence on people outside of the family. If your spouse is been guilty of sexual violence on someone other than you, this section provides for an opportunity to bring that to court as part of your case.

Sexual violence performed on your children by your co-parent is **always** something that you will report to your lawyer and to the judge. It is never excusable and never explainable. Any episode of sexual violence performed on the children would be something that I would consider fatal as far as the claim for custody or visitation with the children.

Child abuse is another tough issue to bring to court. There are families which condone moderate corporal punishment and families that don't. If your family has been one of those that has used moderate corporal punishment for disciplinary purposes, it's going to be very difficult to make a case for child abuse when the evidence may show that you have done it yourself or that you have allowed your partner to do it in the past. Anything that goes further than moderate corporal punishment is going to be found to be child abuse in any event. Usually the determining factor on child abuse is whether or not the corporal punishment leaves a mark that can be seen hours later or the next day. Don't rely on this description too heavily, however. There are judges who have a personal aversion to any sort of corporal punishment on a child and can be convinced that **any** touching for disciplinary purposes is child abuse. The best way to avoid any problems in this regard is to keep your hands off the kids no matter how tempting it is. Even if your family has utilized corporal punishment in the past, you can rest assured that your ex will object to it if you do it after the separation.

Child abandonment and neglect are pretty easy to define and to prove. I'm not going to get too deeply into this because they're both fairly self-explanatory. I will say that having a forgetful moment and accidentally leaving one of the kids at the ball field for twenty minutes is probably not going to be found abandonment or neglect. Leaving the child at home overnight while you go fishing with your buddies or go drinking with your girlfriends could be found to be abandonment or neglect. Generally, the cutoff on leaving kids alone is age twelve and in some cases even older if you're going to leave them overnight. The best way to avoid a problem with this is to discuss it with your ex and make sure you're both on the same page as far as leaving the kids alone and for how long. This is another situation where handwritten notes or e-mails are just about mandatory.

The final sentence of this section indicates that it doesn't matter whether an action for criminal or civil liability for any of these issues has been brought are not. The provisions don't express any importance to whether or not you or your spouse has brought another or separate action in court for alleged violations.

12. Evidence that either parent has knowingly provided false information to the court regarding any prior or pending action regarding domestic violence, sexual violence, child abuse, child abandonment, or child neglect.

This is why I have warned you again and again about making false or unprovable allegations concerning domestic violence, etc. In many states there are specific factors such as the one we are discussing now which provide for the judge to determine if either parent has made a false statement to any court about any of these actions. The bad part about this is that if you have made a claim of domestic violence, for example, and some judge has found your spouse not guilty, you might be accused of giving false information in a prior action (and probably will).

I think at this point it's probably best to go into exactly what domestic violence is and what it's probably not. Domestic violence can be described in most cases as either an assault or battery. These are legal terms so I will give you a description of what they both are and what they probably aren't.

ASSAULT. Generally speaking, an assault is a threat to do violence coupled with present ability to carry out the threat. This means that if a person raises his or her hand with a clenched fist and threatens violence **and** is close enough to the other person to carry out the threat, then an assault is probably committed. The threat to do violence must be immediate and cannot be in the future. The threat made in the future is not an assault. For example, if I say "I'm gonna beat you if you take my car out of the driveway again," that's probably not an assault. However, if I say "I'm gonna beat you for taking my car out of the driveway" and I'm holding a shovel over my head close enough to hit you with it, that probably is an assault.

An assault is **not** a raised voice during an argument. A raised voice containing a threat coupled with an immediate ability to carry out the threat is an assault.

BATTERY. A battery is any unlawful, offensive, or unwanted touching. A battery can be a slap, a punch, a shove, or it can be throwing something at someone or even slamming a door on one's foot. A battery is not a defensive shoving, pushing, or punching. This is all open to interpretation by a judge, however.

I once represented a friend who was getting a divorce. He took some proof photographs to the ball field to show his ex. His intent was to get her feelings on which of the photographs they should order. She took all of the photographs and began walking away. He reached out and touched her arm and told her that she couldn't have the photographs but that she was to pick some so that he can order them. Everyone at the ball field agreed that when he touched her elbow there was no force involved nor was there any harsh language. His ex went straight to her car and called the police. My friend was found guilty of spouse battery. The way to avoid this is not to touch your ex **at all**. Frankly, as I'm sitting here I can think of no good reason that you would need to touch your ex while your divorce is going on.

I have zero patience for someone who commits spouse battery or spousal abuse. Judges don't have any patience for it either. Likewise, I have zero patience for anyone who will stay in a relationship where there is spousal abuse and I have seen situations where judges have disregarded testimony and evidence of spousal abuse because it had become such a routine part of the parties' relationship. Spouse abuse is also known as domestic violence, particularly when the parties share a residence but are not married. To some cops and to some judges, the terms are interchangeable.

A claim made that alleges spousal abuse, domestic violence, child abuse or any form of child abandonment or neglect changes the lives of everyone involved almost instantly. It doesn't matter whether the claim is true or not. If the claim is true, it changes the lives of the victims forever for the better. If the claim is not true it changes the relationship of all the parties for the worse. A spouse or partner that makes a false claim against another spouse can no longer be trusted in the eyes of the spouse against which the claim is made, and it will change the relationship of both of the spouses with the children. If a judge ever feels that a claim of spousal abuse is false, the judge will consider the person making the claim to be untruthful about everything from that point forward.

The reason why I have continued to warn you about making false claims or unprovable claims is that the vast majority of judges understand the life-altering consequences surrounding these claims and the effects they have on every family dynamic.

13. The capacity and disposition of each parent to protect the child from the ongoing litigation as demonstrated by not discussing the litigation with the child, not sharing documents or electronic media related to the litigation with the child, and refraining from disparaging comments about the other parent to the child.

This is actually two things but they've been lumped together in some statutes. I'm going to take them up separately.

As I said before, most judges are very reluctant to have the children involved in these cases at all. This provision specifically provides for a determination of which parent does the better job of restraining themselves when it's so difficult to do so.

By their nature, children are extremely inquisitive and realize that something is different and possibly changing about their environment. They will naturally want to know what's going on. Most parents whom I know are pretty open with their kids and routinely explain things to them, even things that are sometimes difficult for them to understand. You must work to keep from doing what comes naturally in this regard. I explained to you in an earlier provision about the kids coming into contact with what is written in the petition and the counter petition. That's why you keep what you say and those items brief and to the point. About the only things that the kids should know about the divorce is (1) it's happening, and (2) it's not their fault. Aside from that, you must try as hard as you can to keep the kids from knowing what's been said, what the status of the process is, and how it may affect them. Sooner or later the kids will have to find out what's going on in their lives. You and your ex, hopefully, will be able to get together long enough to have a conversation with the children about the next phase of their lives and how these events are going to play out. This is going to be one of the most difficult times in the process. You must not be the one, however, to bring the kids into it. Even if your ex starts telling the kids details of what's going on, you have to resist. This is not one of the bigger issues that a judge is going to base his decision on, but in each one of these circumstances, you have to think that it may be the tipping point. Don't fall into the trap.

The second part of this is sometimes even more difficult than the first. You must at all times refrain for making disparaging remarks about your ex-spouse or co-parent. Although you may think in the spur of the moment that it may feel good to do so, absolutely nothing good can come of it. First and foremost, even though you think the children are on your side and will keep your secret, everything you say will get back to your ex-spouse and ultimately to the judge. You will be **so** tempted to respond to what the children report to you. It may even seem at times that you're doing the children a great disservice by not responding. You have to remember at all times, however, that your co-parent is also someone whom the children love and respect, even if you don't. The things you say about them will be remembered by the children for as long as they live and they will remember every insult and name you call your ex-spouse. In a judge's eyes, the berating of the ex is an attempt by you to alienate the kids from your co-parent and is probably a violation of factor 1, "which will be the one to give the other the most time with the kids."

So there are both legal and personal reasons for both of these extremely difficult prohibitions. I can't stress strongly enough how important these are personally. As I say, they may not be as important as some of the other factors to the judge, but they may be the tipping point when added on to the other factors.

14. The particular parenting tasks customarily performed by each parent and the division of parental responsibilities before the institution of litigation and during the pending litigation, including the extent to which parenting responsibilities were undertaken by third parties.

This one is pretty self-explanatory. You can, however, work on this one during the course of the proceedings. I'll go into that later.

The particular parenting tasks that this section is talking about can be as simple as haircuts or as difficult as helping with homework. What this means is that the judge will accept testimony and evidence with regard to which of you might have been the person to do things such as take the child to the doctor or dentist, help with homework, take the child to football or cheerleading practice and the hundreds of other duties that parents undertake during the course of the week for the children. If you have never been the parent who does these sorts of things, at this moment you're at a pretty distinct disadvantage. This is a kind of a big issue with some judges. The fact that you may have been the one to perform all of these tasks on a weekly basis, or maybe you're the one who performed few if any of them, could help the judge decide where the kids should be placed and who may be the one who would be more likely to carry out these weekly chores in the future. If there had been a pretty distinct and even division of these weekly or daily chores, you're probably just about equal on the strength of this evidence. Frankly, have to confess I've never seen a family dynamic where these chores were equally divided. Remember, too, that if your ex has never done any of these things and now wants to do some, you should let him or her try it. If you don't, you may be seen as a person who wants to isolate the kids from the other parent. If he or she can't keep up or disappoints the child, that's evidence. The flip side is the parent who has never tried any of these jobs in the past and still doesn't try. That parent has a *future* history as a non-participant and will struggle to get custody or significant visitation.

If you have never been the one to take the kids to the doctor, to cheerleading or football practice, or to the department store for clothing, now is the time for you to start. If you are not prepared to take on these tasks during the pendency of your divorce and custody trial, the judge may determine that possibly you are not the one who can be relied upon to make sure there is continuity in the lives of the children after the divorce is final. Even if you have never been the one to do it in the past, many divorce actions that involve custody can go on for months and you can create a **new** history for that period of months before the judge has to make a decision. If you have been thinking of enrolling a child in tutoring classes or even batting practice, this may be the time for you to start volunteering. The more you show the judge in this regard, the stronger your evidence will be and the more likely you will be to win this fight. Careful, if you start and then quit participating, it can be worse than if you never did it at all.

The last part of this section deals with the specific parenting chores that were undertaken by third parties. A third party in this regard deals with people who have acted for you in the position of the parent. This may be a nanny, grandparents, older adult siblings, or any other people who actually took care of some of these duties for the kids.

If you and your spouse typically worked outside of the home at regular jobs, it is possible there may have been third-party people doing some of these duties. If it was customary to have a housekeeper or a nanny during the course of your marriage or your relationship, maybe the housekeeper of the nanny performed some of those duties. Housekeepers and nannies are typically difficult to keep after a divorce or breakup happens. Having that extra expense in the household can be extremely difficult when there's only one parent in the residence. It may be, however, that this is the sort of lifestyle you and your co-parent had chosen and possibly want to keep after the relationship is over. If that is the case and both of you agree to it, the existence of the nanny or housekeeper probably is not going to affect the outcome of the decision one way or another. If you recognize that keeping the nanny is not possible in the post-breakup environment, you may want to take these responsibilities on right away to create the new history for the judge. Think this over, however. It's difficult to get off work on a predictable basis at three o'clock to pick up the children and take them directly to a practice that may be across town.

The real problem in this section develops when these third-party people are part of an extended family support group. If your co-parent has parents, siblings, aunts, uncles, or cousins who routinely are involved in the children's lives and it is desirable to keep them, it may be a difficult proposition for you to overcome the judge's natural tendency to leave these support groups in place. Obviously if it's your parents or cousins who are performing these tasks, you should encourage leaving the systems in place because this will be something the judge will want to leave as part of the kids' ordinary routine. Judges are well aware that, for the most part, people like grandparents, cousins, and others don't have the ability to go to court and ask for time with the children. They **are** a part of the usual support system for one parent or both, which is good. Judges also know that kids over the course of years become extremely attached to and look forward to the time they spend with grandparents, even if it's only cheerleading practice once a week. My experience is that the judges very rarely want to break up this routine. Judges also know that after the divorce and custody orders are entered, grandparents may be excluded from doing these sorts of things if they're not the parents of the custodial spouse. Extended family and support groups are good for lots of reasons. Men are usually not as good as women at cultivating them. They should start!

15. The developmental stages and needs of the child and the demonstrated capacity and disposition of each parent to meet the child's developmental needs.

If your children are really young, there may be one of you who is better at dealing with an infant or a particularly young child than the other is. Likewise, if your child is really young and you have no other children, you're really in for some exciting times as the kids grow older.

Young girls develop emotionally differently than young boys do. The timing is different, the intensity is different, and the stages are different.

The judge has to try to determine, based on what you tell him or her and also based on his own experience, the best placement for the child based on his or her developmental stages. The demonstrated capacity and disposition between you and your ex is a tough one for the judge to determine. It's all going to come down to your testimony and possibly the testimony of witnesses as to which of you may be the better person in your child's or children's developmental stage to deal with the problems and challenges that kids face as they grow up.

A lot of people think that the way to prove this to a judge is to be willing to take the child or children to counseling as they go through these life-altering and sometimes terrible changes. While that is a valid option, my suggestion is that you should be reading everything you can about the child's developmental stages, possibly even get counseling for yourself on how to deal with it. You will want to keep a list of books or articles you have read and notes you've taken when talking to a counselor (possibly child psychologist) about what to do and how to act with the children. This is going to exhibit to the judge your demonstrated capacity and disposition on trial day. Remember, you should be researching not only your child's current developmental stage but also the next one so that you can show the judge you're a step ahead of the problems as they occur. This is a real opportunity to create that *future* history.

16. Any other factor that is relevant to the determination of a specific parenting plan, including the time-sharing schedule.

I have been telling you as we went along that the court can consider other factors not specifically set out in your state's statute. Generally, you will have a provision either exactly like this or very similar to this item 16 which will give the judge the ability to utilize other factors outside the set rules. Some states have specific language with regard to a parent's awareness of the circumstances of the minor child including the child's friends, teachers, medical care providers, daily activities, and favorite things. We have already been over those, and I hope by now you know that you should be really conversant with those them at all times during the course of the litigation. Some statutes contain a specific section on constant routine, discipline, and daily schedules for homework meals and bedtime. Since we've already been over those items as well, I hope you have figured those into the factors above.

There can also be specific statutes or specific parts of statutes which require parents to maintain a drug- or substance-free environment for the child. In my mind, that goes without saying. I would be remiss, however, if I didn't remind you at this point under the all-inclusive item 16.

You will have to determine if your state has any of these specific factors that are in addition to the ones in this chapter. I have known some state statutes to require the judge to take into consideration matters such as:

1. Any recommendation by court-appointed custody evaluator or guardian ad litem.

2. Any evidence of substance abuse by either parent, whether or not it was in the presence of the children.

3. The home, school, and community record and history of the child.

4. Any criminal history by either parent.

5. Any evidence of family violence or sexual, mental, or physical child abuse by either parent (not specifically having to do with the children who are the subject of the current custody and visitation matter).

You also have to remember that each individual state can establish its own order of importance of these provisions, so you need to find out from your attorney the exact order in which they appear in the state statutes. Sometimes the most important ones will be identified as of primary importance so you should probably spend most of your time gathering proof of those.

Finally, a word about any new friends that you may make.

Your soon-to-be ex has a right to know whom the child is spending time with. Most single men and women I know insist on a wide-spectrum STD test on potential partners before the relationship goes too far since between twenty-five and forty percent of sexually active adults in this country has some sort of STD. Since your co-parent can and probably will investigate your new friend when they find out that the kids are spending time with him or her, don't you think you should, too? It may even give your co-parent some degree of confidence in your choices if you are able to state with a degree of certainty that your new friend has no criminal history and has never been accused of domestic violence. The last thing you want to find out is that your new boyfriend or girlfriend has one of these problems in a trial setting. Obviously, the converse is true. When your co-parent becomes socially active and starts introducing the kids to his or her new friend, you have a right to find out who that person is and if they have any problems in their past that may cause you concern.

6

The Discovery Process

What is discovery?

Discovery, broadly speaking, is the process through which the parties to a lawsuit gain access to and learn about information they need to either prove or disprove the counts and the things that are said in the original and all supplemental pleadings and papers filed by the plaintiff or defendant. In layman's terms, this means the process by which you gain information either from your ex, his or her witnesses, or his or her documents. I discussed this generally in *Divorce and Conquer*, but I realize some people may not have read it. So I'm going to go into specific discovery techniques here with an emphasis on custody and visitation issues.

Discovery usually takes three forms. There is an oral form which is the actual statements from witnesses and parties. There is the written form which is questions posed to the opposite party or to witnesses in a document that requires a written response. Finally, there is the documentary form which is a request for the production of documents such as tax returns, pay or compensation statements, or any other document that you can think of.

WRITTEN DISCOVERY

Written discovery is usually in one of two forms. The first and the most widely used is a document called "interrogatories." Interrogatories are written questions proposed from one party to another or from one party to a witness always in written form that can be either questions specifically authorized by statute or questions that are uniquely made up by one party's attorney or other. For the most part, the first set of interrogatories sent in any lawsuit are general and request general information such as name, address, Social Security number, bank account numbers, etc. Along with these general interrogatories may be subheadings asking the person filling out the interrogatories whether or not they have the bank statements, etc., mentioned in the main body of the question. Special interrogatories are usually identified as such and are special questions generally tailor-made for the nature of the lawsuit you're involved with.

Special interrogatories regarding custody and visitation cases can ask specific questions not covered in the general interrogatories. As an example, a special interrogatory might ask if you have ever been arrested or convicted of a crime. If the answer is yes, there could be a follow-up or second part of the question which asks you to describe the circumstances of the arrest or conviction. The follow-up questions may ask for the date and place of the arrest also. You could assume at that point that the attorney will get a copy of the arrest record and any court proceedings that may have come as a result of the arrest.

Special interrogatories can get very involved and can ask for very small details concerning the inquiry. There is generally a limit to the numbers of interrogatories that can be asked without permission of the court, however. Your lawyer will tell you when you have answered enough interrogatories.

REQUESTS FOR ADMISSIONS

A "request for admissions" is usually something that is provided for in the Rules of Court in every state. It is exactly what it sounds like. Usually the request for admissions will be in the same format as the interrogatories, but the responses will be limited to admitting the question or denying the question.

Primarily the request for admissions is used to limit the number of witnesses necessary to prove small or undeniable facts. For example, you could get a request for admissions that ask you to "admit or deny that you were convicted of armed robbery in March of 2005." Another request for admissions could be "admit or deny that you were married to your wife in January 1999 and separated in April 2005." You can probably tell that a request for admissions is a valuable tool. Not only does it limit the proof necessary for trial purposes, but it can also limit the number of witnesses necessary to testify about smaller or undisputed facts.

The request for admissions can also be used to get a set of answers to difficult or disputed facts as well. For example, you could receive a request for admissions that asks "admit or deny that you had a sexual relationship with John Doe during the months of January and February 2005." Of course, answering a question like this in the positive is difficult, but it may just save your friend John from having to come to court and be cross-examined.

Remember, it's a terrible idea to lie during any phase of the court proceeding. If you lie on interrogatories or on a request for admissions and the other attorney proves that you're lying, the results can be catastrophic for a number different reasons. First, you'll be a liar in the eyes of the judge from that point forward. Second, it may expose you to an award of attorneys' fees for unnecessary litigation. A competent and ethical attorney will never allow you to lie while he or she knows of it. An attorney who encourages you to lie is not someone you want to be associated with. Remember, an attorney who tells you to lie will also lie about you at some point.

Lastly, a request for admissions that goes unanswered passed the time for responses that is set out in the rules is deemed to be admitted. This is about the only place in discovery that silence is an answer. This means that if you don't answer in time, you have answered yes.

FINANCIAL AFFIDAVIT

The last form of written discovery that you are going to see is the standard financial affidavit. The standard financial affidavit is a one- to possibly six-page document that will ask you to provide your monthly expenses in writing. The financial affidavit will usually contain more requests than there are expenses. For example, most form financial affidavits that I have seen have a request for a monthly expense that you may have for pet care, pet food, and/or pet grooming. If you don't have a pet, obviously you don't have these expenses. Everyone, or almost everyone, will have an expense for rent or mortgage, electricity, water, telephone, etc. You should be extremely careful about being accurate on this financial affidavit. It is possible to change it at a later date, but you'll have to explain the reason for the change. The financial affidavit will also ask for your monthly income figures. If you don't have a predictable monthly income, you may be forced to calculate it based on last year's income or possibly this year's income that you have or may receive. Remember, a month is 4.3 weeks so if you are paid weekly, you must multiply your income by 4.3 in order to get an accurate monthly amount. If you're paid every two weeks, the best way to calculate your income is simply to take your annual pay and divide by 12. Bonuses, comp time, and some benefits like a take-home car are required to be included in your income in many jurisdictions. You should probably go over your financial affidavit with your lawyer or your lawyer's paralegal before signing the final draft to be sent to the other side. The financial affidavit is necessary in cases of custody and visitation for purposes of calculating child support and sometimes attorney's fees.

ORAL DISCOVERY

Oral discovery, for the most part, is in the form of depositions. The deposition is a sworn statement taken in an "out of court" proceeding before a court reporter and/or sometimes a videographer. The court reporter or videographer (sometimes both) are there to record your responses or witnesses responses to questions asked by the attorney. Generally, a deposition will be scheduled far enough in advance that both you and your attorney can attend or schedule your attendance if you are the person who is the subject of the deposition. If your attorney is taking the deposition of your soon-to-be ex or co-parent, you may or may not want to go, sometimes depending on the level of acrimony involved in the case.

An oral examination, or deposition, can be extremely wide ranging and the questions asked are almost limitless. The only true limits on the questions that may come up in a deposition are those that are protected by some "privilege." These privileges include your Fifth Amendment privilege against self-incrimination, doctor-patient privilege, parishioner and clergy privilege, and attorney-client privilege. In some states there is a privilege against testifying against your spouse, but generally in a divorce proceeding everybody waives that one. In custody and visitation proceedings, the judge may order a person to testify in violation of his or her Fifth Amendment privilege sometimes in order to protect the interests of the children. Some judges do this routinely, and some judges will not do it at all. Your lawyer is just going to have to tell you which kind of judge you have. Some are of the opinion that the Fifth Amendment privilege is more important than anything, and some believe that the best interests of the children are more important.

I mentioned earlier that if your lawyer is taking your ex's deposition, you may not want to go. I found that it was easier for me to convince an ex-spouse to relax in a deposition if my client wasn't there. It seems as though most people are very guarded and careful in what they say if their ex-spouse or co-parent is sitting across from them.

The deposition can be very long, very short, or anything in between. Some attorneys spend days questioning ex-spouses and co-parents.

You should spend some time with your attorney before your deposition getting ready for the questions you may be asked. This is one place where it's really important that you have been honest and open with your attorney before you even go to the deposition.

Likewise, you should spend some time helping your attorney prepare for the deposition of your spouse or co-parent. It may even be a good idea for the two of you to go over the questions that he or she will be asking so that you can help to create even more questions or help your attorney to design a line of questioning.

The deposition is a place where an attorney gets a feeling for the ability of a witness or client to speak under pressure. It's also an opportunity for an attorney to get a feeling for how a witness or client may act when they're attempting to conceal something. Your demeanor during your deposition should transmit to the court reporter and the other attorney that you are telling the truth and that you're not trying to conceal anything.

Witnesses who are not parties to the case can also be the subject of a deposition. People who know you or know something about you--your doctor, your accountant, or anyone who may have pertinent information concerning the custody and visitation of your kids can be called as a witness to give a deposition, as well as testify in court. The rules concerning witnesses are just about the same as the ones concerning your testimony. But witnesses can always be asked to talk about what you might've said to them or what you might have said in their presence. You should spend some time before the deposition of any witness with your lawyer going over things that most certainly will be said, or might be said, during the deposition of that witness.

Remember, if you take your mother, father, or new boyfriend to any meeting with your lawyer, they can be called to testify about what was said in their presence because talking to a lawyer in the presence of any third party is a waiver of attorney-client privilege. You may sometimes be able to work this in your favor, however. I have on occasion, just for humor purposes, planted some information with witnesses who came to interviews or meetings with clients. Whenever I knew that an attorney was going to ask a witness (mother, father, brother) if they had been in a meeting between my client and me, I would say "your husband (John) has proven himself to be a complete psychopathic liar and his lawyer is a total jerk (not the word I used). But we don't want him to know about all the stuff that we have on his business and his girlfriend." The first part obviously was just my sense of humor. The second part, however, about the business and the girlfriend may induce a less than honest person to think we knew more than we did.

Along the same line of thinking, you have to remember that anything you might say to your friends, siblings, or any relationship is a fair question for the other lawyer to ask you and also is a fair question to ask whomever you said it to. I know it's tough, but you have to think about this even when you need to vent to somebody you trust. They may be your best friend, but they can be a devastating witness against you, too.

Depositions of expert and professional witnesses like accountants, appraisers, and doctors can take hours to complete. You have to remember at all times that anything you say to these people is also fair game for questioning by the other attorney. My advice is to keep your relationship with any of these professionals on a strictly professional basis and only talk about what is necessary to give them the information they need.

DOCUMENTARY DISCOVERY

The general heading "documentary discovery" is the search for and the production of documents pursuant to a request by the other party or something that is required by the Rules of Court in your state or area. Documents include anything that might be on paper, electronically stored, either on your computer or some other computer, and may include documents in the possession of your lawyer or accountant or possibly your banker.

The latest trend in discovery is to get possession of and examine your electronic devices. Your phone, blackberry, etc., are all items that can be subpoenaed and dumped for information and evidence. Be careful.

RULES CONCERNING MANDATORY DISCLOSURE

Many jurisdictions, and I may even say most jurisdictions, currently have some rules concerning mandatory disclosure of documents without a request. By that I mean there may be a rule (and probably is) concerning the documents that are to be provided to you and by you in a lawsuit involving custody and visitation. The reason for this is that, for the most part, actions including custody and visitation also include child support requests, and therefore require financial documentation to be exchanged. These are documents that you must give your ex or his or her lawyer without even being asked.

The mandatory disclosure rules can be slightly different in each jurisdiction but, for the most part, will include the following:

(1) The rule will probably require you to file a financial affidavit that substantially follows the form outlined or specified in the rules or the administrative orders in your area.

(2) You will probably be required to provide all federal and state tax returns along with any gift tax or intangible property tax return you may have filed over the last year, and it sometimes may ask for three years.

(3) You will have to, under most circumstances, provide pay stubs for the last three months along with your W–2, 1099, or

K–1 statement for the prior year or any combination of those items that will adequately inform the other party as to your income both for the current year and the year before.

(4) You may be required to provide a statement identifying all sources of income including the ones from item three above but specifically any additional sources of income you may have had for the prior year and the current year.

(5) You may be required to provide any and all loan applications you filled out or presented to a lender in the last one to three years, including any financial affidavit that was attached or you were required to fill out along with the loan application. (This is to find out what you tell others about your income.)

(6) If you have bought or sold any real property or personal property during the last year, you may be required to produce deeds you signed or received for the sale of real property and titles which you signed or received evidencing the sale of personal property. There may be a lower limit on the personal property aspect of this. That means that if you sold used furniture for a hundred dollars, you may not be responsible for having documentation for it, but if you sold the boat for $5000, you probably will be responsible for the documentation.

(7) You will have to produce any statements concerning brokerage accounts, and usually checking accounts for the last six months or the latest statement in case of an account that only produces statements annually.

(8) You may be responsible for producing statements from any profit-sharing accounts that you have, 401(k)s, IRAs, or any retirement accounts you may have or be eligible for.

(9) There may be a requirement that you produce the declaration pages or evidence of cash value in any life insurance policy you

may have including any loans you have made taking money from any life insurance policy for the last three years.

(10) The rules may require you to produce copies of any promissory notes either to or from you as evidence of any money you have borrowed or you have lent someone else for the past three years.

(11) You will probably be required to produce a written copy of any premarital agreements you have with your spouse if you are married. Some rules say that if there is no premarital agreement, there may be other evidence of an agreement to limit or waive support. In that case, you would be required to produce any documents or evidence that he or she would intend to use to prove this waiver.

(12) You would also probably be asked to produce any contracts or final judgments ordering you to pay or ordering some third party to pay you child support or alimony.

The reason most states have adopted these mandatory disclosure rules is so that all parties can have access to what the legislatures considered to be the minimum amount of information necessary for one person or another to make a decision on how much child support or alimony should be paid or received. If your family is such that you both receive a paycheck on the weekly or monthly basis, under the vast majority of circumstances, the information required under these mandatory disclosure rules will be sufficient to give you or your co-parent the information necessary to calculate child support.

If your financial situation or the financial situation of your co-parent is not as easy as that or the mandatory disclosure rules do not call for the exchange of enough information, there are other things your lawyer can do to get more financial information and documentation.

SUBPOENA DUCES TECUM

I guess most people know and understand what a subpoena is. For the most part, a subpoena is a command by the court to appear for one reason or another. It might be to give evidence or testimony or it could be to produce documents. The *Duces Tecum* part of the subpoena in this regard is a Latin phrase which roughly means "bring it with you." The "bring it with you" part refers to documents and sometimes tangible evidence or objects that may be involved in a lawsuit or criminal prosecution. For our purposes, it is generally used on witnesses (not parties to the lawsuit) to command them to come to a deposition or to a hearing to give evidence and to bring with them some document or set of documents so that the lawyer who has issued the subpoena can have the person and the documents in the same place at the same time. When the person (it could be a banker, stockbroker, corporate representative, or any other person) arrives with the documents, the attorney can then look at the documents and question the person about the documents at the same time. Generally the attorney will then make copies of the documents that have been brought so that they can be used at a later time in evidence at a hearing or trial. The subpoena could also be used to get a look at a gun or coin collection or any other tangible object.

REQUEST FOR PRODUCTION OF DOCUMENTS

A request for production of documents is a specifically designed request for only certain documents which may be necessary in some cases involving custody and visitation and indirectly child support. A request for production of documents can be addressed to a banker, stockbroker, or any other person who may be in possession of the requested or desired documents to be produced generally at the lawyer's office requesting. Documents can also be requested from the police department, the state, and even of the federal government. The nature of the request can be anything from criminal records, financial records, corporate records, or anything else that you can imagine. There has to be some sort of reasonable connection, however, between the case as framed by the pleadings (the lawsuit) and the documents themselves.

Obviously, criminal records might be used to establish one party or the other's criminal history. Hospital or psychological records would be used to establish the physical or mental health of one party or the other. Records from the Department of State might be used to establish the existence of a Corporation or some other registered company in the name of one or the other co-parents. Records from the Department of Transportation might be used to establish ownership of vehicles or maybe even the driving record of one or the other. You can see now what a powerful tool the request for production of documents can be.

Go back now to the first part of this chapter and look at the request for admissions. If the other party denies having been convicted of a DUI, the lawyer can simply do a request for production of documents from the Department of Transportation and get the DUI conviction placed into the trial record along with the other party's denial. This establishes two things. The other party was convicted of DUI, and he or she lied about it. Win-win!

The discovery tools that we talked about in this chapter and sometimes the combination of them in your lawyer's hands can be the difference between winning and losing your custody and visitation case. You may wonder at times why he or she wants to do so many of these things, but maybe you've got a better sense now of why they are so varied.

Each one of these discovery devices has its own time limits for responses or answers, usually established by the statute or the rules in your state or in your jurisdiction. If you're reading this before you even go to see an attorney, you should go back to the list of items included on the possible mandatory production rule and gather them before you even make the first appointment. You can be well ahead of the game if you do that. In any event, if you have already started your case or you have been drawn into a case, do not neglect to produce the documents requested on a timely basis or tell your attorney that the documents included in the list here he or she has asked you for are not available to you quickly so the proper responses can be delivered to the other lawyer.

Sometimes the documents and evidence don't even exist. For example, you probably don't have **all** of the following: a 401K, a retirement account, a pension, profit sharing, and a brokerage account. If you have possibly only one out of the four, you're only required to produce the documents and evidence surrounding the one that you have. Likewise, you probably don't have a W-2 and 1099. You probably only have one of the two. You're only required to produce the one that you have or the one that you can get your hands on. You do not have to manufacture anything to satisfy these document requests.

Most states either have case law or rules, however, that say if the documents requested are in your possession, your banker's possession, your lawyer's possession, your broker's possession, or any other party who works directly for you, then you should produce them. Don't fall under the trap of saying "I don't have the stuff" only to find out that the judge might award the other party attorney's fees because they have to send subpoenas to these people. It only wastes time and money. Be sure to talk to your attorney about this.

Finally, all discovery requests come with a time limit for responses. I can't say this too much or too strongly. The penalties for not responding on time can range from very small to very severe. In the case of the "request for admissions," if you go over the allotted time for the response, the questions are presumed answered "YES" for all purposes. If you don't file a response to the mandatory discovery, in some jurisdictions, both you and your lawyer can be responsible for your co-parent's attorney's fees if there is a hearing on your late answers. In some extreme cases, the judge can "strike your pleadings," which is like a death sentence for your lawsuit. If your pleadings are stricken, you may have no right to ask for anything from the judge and you are left purely defensive.

7

Hearings that May Occur Before the Trial

First, let's establish just what a hearing is. A hearing is a formal meeting between you and your lawyer and your co-parent and his or her lawyer with the judge. It might be in the judge's chambers (office), in a small hearing room, or in the large court room. A hearing can be requested by either party for many reasons but always require some action by the judge. Hearings may be formal or informal, long or short, special or routine. Hearings can be specially scheduled or "cattle call." Some judges have short hearings (maybe ten minutes or less) on a "first come, first served" basis for an hour or two every week. A trial is always a hearing (sometimes called a final hearing), but not all hearings are trials.

Hearings are most often the result of one or the other of the attorneys filing what's called a *motion*. A motion is a paper filed in court that asks the judge to take notice of a set of facts or actions and do something about them. After the paper is filed in the clerk's office, it is served or delivered on the other attorney or, if the other party is unrepresented by an attorney, it may be served directly on the person. After that, the hearing is scheduled and both parties and their attorneys appear before the judge so that the judge can be aware of what is in the motion and take action as the judge may think is necessary.

In this chapter I'll discuss what kind of hearings you may encounter while you're waiting for your trial. This is not a completely exhaustive list and there may be others that aren't mentioned. I'm trying to go over the ones that are most often part of the custody and visitation proceeding.

THE DOMESTIC VIOLENCE HEARING

According to my completely unscientific experience during my practice, about one in seven divorce cases seem to have an element, or at least an alleged element, of domestic violence. Most, if not all medium to large counties, circuits, or districts have courts and judges who are specifically assigned to handle domestic violence cases. I think it's impossible to tell whether the number of domestic violence cases has gone up significantly in the last thirty years or whether the alleged domestic violence is just being reported a lot more now. In either case, it seems to be a subject that courts are preoccupied with and police agencies are very sensitive about. Domestic violence hearings can be criminal or civil and the courts take them **much** more seriously today than in the past.

A domestic violence complaint is initiated by the person who feels as though he or she is the victim of domestic violence. In most situations, the victim has to go to the courthouse in the county, circuit, or district where he or she lives to fill out an affidavit that will be attached to a petition for a domestic violence restraining order or injunction. The affidavit and petition then go to a "duty judge" who examines the affidavit of the petition to see if on its face it makes a case for a restraining order or injunction. Restraining orders and injunctions, without a hearing involving the person against whom they are sought, are what are known in the legal world as "extraordinary remedies." Extraordinary remedies are supposed to be issued only in dire circumstances, when there is no other legal choice and when the chance of damage or continued damage requires immediate action. The reality is that almost all domestic violence affidavits and petitions are granted on a temporary basis. The courts and police departments are reluctant to be blamed for anyone being injured because of their lack of action. For this reason most of these temporary injunctions or temporary restraining orders are granted.

A temporary restraining order or injunction stays in place until a hearing on the matter can be accomplished in a court of competent jurisdiction. In most cases, the definition of a court of competent jurisdiction means a court that is assigned to have hearings on domestic violence issues. For the most part, the hearings happen within a week or ten days of the issuance of the restraining order or injunction. The law usually requires a temporary order or injunction that has been entered against a person who was not in court to defend him or herself to be called up for a full hearing very quickly. Very quickly in legal terms can be a set number of days if the statute specifies it, or a week or ten days if it does not.

The restraining order that we talked about usually orders the respondent (the person against whom the domestic violence petition is directed) to get out of the house immediately and have no contact with the complaining witness. A normal provision of these things gives the respondent a few hours to get his or her clothes and small personal articles out of the house. The respondent has to find a place to live for the intervening week or ten days and have no contact with the person who swore to the petition. This also means that the respondent has no contact with his or her children for that intervening ten days. Generally there is no provision for even telephone contact with the children during that time. You can see how extreme and devastating one of these temporary orders can be.

Within a week or ten days, the hearing on the domestic violence restraining order occurs and the judge either extends it for a year or indefinitely or dismisses it. The judge has the ability to modify the restraining order with either more or less restrictions after the hearing. The hearing on the restraining order is attended by both parties, the person making the complaint and the person against whom the complaint is made, and any witnesses they want to bring. Both parties can hire a lawyer if they want and bring other evidence including telephone records, hospital records, witnesses, etc.

Domestic violence hearings can be of a criminal nature as well. In those cases, the person making the complaint calls the police after the violence happens. The police either arrest the person complained of and take him or her to jail or issue a summons (notice to appear, like a traffic ticket). The case then moves through the system like an ordinary criminal case. The charge can be a misdemeanor or felony usually depending on the injuries that the complaining person has suffered. People who are convicted of criminal domestic violence can get anything from a fine up to years in jail as a sentence.

As you were reading chapter 5, I'm sure you noticed that most jurisdictions require divorce judges to take into account any evidence of domestic violence against a spouse or co-parent and also any evidence of unfounded allegations of domestic violence against a spouse or co-parent. In addition to being a life-altering event just by the very nature of the domestic violence proceeding, you can understand now why the claim of or a finding of guilt in a domestic violence hearing can be of supreme importance during a custody and visitation proceeding. That is why I have continuously said that you should be extremely careful about making a claim of domestic violence against a co-parent and making sure that what is happening between you truly is domestic violence before you make the claim. A rash desire to get a spouse out of the house "at all costs" can bring with it a life of distrust and horrible consequences.

Once again, arguing with raised voices is probably not domestic violence. Arguing with raised voices coupled with the threat of violence probably is. Any unwanted or illegal touching is probably domestic violence. Any threat of violence coupled with the present ability to carry out the threat is probably domestic violence. This would include slamming the door on someone's foot or possibly damaging the door where someone has gone to take refuge. Frankly, it's all in the eyes of the judge.

Domestic violence hearings can be very short or can take all day depending on the amount and quality of evidence the parties have and are willing to put into the record. In addition to being careful about making a claim of domestic violence, you should be prepared to follow up on it or defend it to the fullest extent of your abilities because it can be of enormous importance later in the custody and visitation trial.

TEMPORARY HEARINGS

Temporary hearings can be requested for almost any purpose you can think of. Typically, a temporary hearing can be for custody and visitation, child support, alimony, attorney's fees, exclusive use and possession of real estate or personal property (like a car), or almost anything else. They are called "temporary hearings" because they are used to get temporary orders during the time that you are waiting for a trial when you get "final" orders.

Temporary orders or judgments concerning child custody and visitation are some of the most frequent and most contentious hearings you can imagine. I have personally conducted temporary hearings that lasted three days. Next to the domestic violence restraining order hearings, the temporary hearing can be the most important of the opening stages of any divorce case or case involving custody and visitation. They can be completely or partially contested and completely or partially agreed upon. Temporary orders on custody and visitation generally last until the final hearing which could be anywhere from a few months to a year depending on the intensity of the litigation that's occurring. You can see why they're so important. If you get a temporary order giving you "temporary" primary custody of the kids and it takes a year to get to the trial, you can make a lot of *future* history during that year. The continuity factor alone (having the kids with you) can be huge.

It is important to parties and for the children that the parents may be able to come together and negotiate at least part of any temporary order or judgment concerning custody and visitation. For example, if the parties can agree that the kids should live with their father (or mother) during the time they're waiting for trial but can't agree on the nature and frequency of visits with the mom, the time necessary for a hearing is at least cut in half.

If the parents can only negotiate small parts of the temporary custody and visitation orders, or they are unable to negotiate any of the temporary custody and visitation scheme, the temporary hearing is where the proof and evidence is presented to the judge regarding your thoughts and your co-parent's thoughts and evidence about where the children should live temporarily (during the course of the lawsuit) and if or how much visitation should be awarded to the other parent during that time. This is a real balancing act because you have to present enough convincing evidence to the judge to grant you the custody and visitation order you want but not turn it into a full-blown trial at the same time. You are really going to have to take your lawyer's advice regarding how much time, evidence, and the number of witnesses that are going to be necessary in order to win the temporary hearing without turning it into something that will take so long to get on the judge's calendar. Sadly, this is the place for you to think into the future as much as possible. You should be asking the judge to make provisions on a temporary basis for Christmas, birthdays, and school vacation day visitations even though you probably believe your custody and visitation case will be over far in advance of those sorts of orders being necessary.

Issues of exclusive use and possession can also come up during custody and visitation matters as part of the custody orders. For example, if mom wants to stay in the house with the kids but dad doesn't want to leave, there might be a hearing or part of a hearing that deals with the issue. As an aside, in the last few years the courts are getting more and more reluctant to order one parent out of the house on a temporary basis without a claim of domestic violence attached to or as part of the request for exclusive use and possession of the house. The theory here is that both parties have equal rights to be in the home with the kids while the lawsuit is going on unless someone in the home is in danger by leaving both parties in the home. My personal opinion is that this is one of the causes of the huge increase in domestic violence filings.

A request for exclusive use and possession of personal property, such as a car, can also be part of a custody and visitation request. Imagine a circumstance where dad is the sole owner of both of the family cars but mom has been driving the SUV for the last three years. Dad may claim possession of both of the cars because of the title ownership when mom clearly needs possession of the SUV for her use and for transportation of the children on a daily basis.

You can see that a temporary hearing is very important and should be taken with the utmost seriousness. All of the sections of chapter 5 should be consulted and, if time permits, you should go into each and every one of those sections with your lawyer and bring them up with the judge during a temporary hearing. The reality is not so simple. Getting a temporary hearing long enough to bring up all of the provisions of chapter 5 could take months. So there is a balancing act that has to be done between your desire to have all of these issues heard and the reality that the more time you request on the judge's calendar the longer it will take to get it. If you add in the fact that you're going to either need to request support during that hearing or defend a support action during that hearing, you can be talking about many hours, and the time delay between your request for hearing time and the time that you actually get the hearing could end up being months.

DISCOVERY MOTIONS AND HEARINGS

I don't think I can remember a trial case that didn't have at least one discovery motion and hearing. The trial case is one that appears to be on schedule and on track to a trial as its ultimate conclusion. Cases that are not on a trial track can also have discovery problems that generate motions and hearings.

The classic discovery hearing is one that seeks to compel answers to interrogatories or requests for production of documents. There can be discovery hearings, however, that seek to compel responses to requests for production of a financial affidavit, attendance at a deposition, or almost anything else.

As I discussed with you earlier, one or both of the attorneys involved in the custody and visitation case will probably file some sort of discovery request. It could be any of the ones that were described in the previous chapters. Each different type of discovery request has, as part of its rule, the time for the answer, response, or production of some information or document. For the most part, lawyers will encourage if not insist that their clients comply with the time limits to avoid a "motion to compel" whatever is requested. The "motion to compel" is the vehicle with which a lawyer seeks to force the other party to comply with the rule on time for compliance. You really want to try to comply with the time limits because sometimes just the filing of a motion to compel can cost you both attorney's fees in your lawyer's office and also attorney's fees in your co-parent's office. Many judges will award attorney's fees just because of the necessity to enforce the rule as far as time of compliance.

There could be some reason for the noncompliance which may excuse, or may not, lateness or refusal to comply with the discovery request. Some of the reasons for excusable noncompliance may be illness (either on your part or your attorney), inability to find or gather the information requested, or in some cases, the request for information or documentation may be found to be too broad in its scope or "unduly burdensome." Refusal or reluctance to comply with a discovery request may also be based on a violation of some other rule or some privilege such as the "attorney-client privilege" or a violation of the Fifth Amendment privilege.

In an earlier chapter, I describe to you the importance of answering the requests for admissions on a timely basis. I'll remind you again. You probably will never receive a motion to compel answers to requests for admissions because if you don't answer in the time allotted, the rule, and the law in most states, says that you have admitted them by not answering them.

The motion itself will be a fairly simple document. It will set out the type of discovery request that is complained of, the time the request was served on you or your co-parent, and the day the response should have been delivered under the rule. The motion will then go on to request that the judge order the compliance with the request within a certain amount of days and the motion could also request an award of attorney's fees because the motion to compel compliance was made necessary by the lateness of the responses or the noncompliance itself.

If the noncompliance is simply due to neglect on your part or the part of an attorney, it's usually settled by an agreement to provide the documents or information within a certain number of days and will not require a hearing. If there is some valid reason or some perceived reason that the responses or the documentation should be delayed or denied, the attorney who wants the delay or doesn't want to produce the documents or information generally has the burden to file something in court before the time for compliance on the original request runs out. This could be something like a motion for "protective order". Most judges feel that if a motion for protective order is not filed within the time allotted for the original compliance, then any complaint about the discovery request is waived. The motion for protective order is just what it sounds like. It asks the judge to make a finding that you don't have to answer the questions in the interrogatories (for example) or produce some documents. The motion for protective order can be used to object to the scheduling of a deposition or many other purposes.

The hearing on a motion to compel discovery is generally fairly quick and easy. The person requesting the information simply proves the delivery of the discovery documents to the other party and then testifies that it wasn't received within the time allotted. The person who is delaying or denying giving the information then has to prove why he or she hasn't done it or why it has to be delayed. For the most part, these only take minutes although I have seen some that took hours simply because of the volume of the requested documents or information. The hearing itself is held in the judge's chambers, a small hearing room, or in open court, depending on the judge's preference.

There can be a lot of gamesmanship involved in these things. For example, a lawyer can't file a motion to compel discovery until the time for the compliance has come and gone. It may take a few days or even a week to schedule a hearing on the motion to compel because of some inability to get the judge's office on the telephone, get the other attorney's office on the telephone, or schedule a time that everyone (your attorney, the other attorney, you, and the judge) has a sufficient amount of time at the same time to have the hearing. This may take a month or more and many times the request is complied with before you can even get in court.

OTHER HEARINGS

There may be other issues that come up that require hearing during the time you're waiting to get to a full-blown trial.

A "motion to sequester" or some other motion to protect personal or real property may come up during the time you're waiting for your trial. It may be called a "motion to prohibit alienation of property" or something else having to do with prohibiting the sale or transfer of personal or real property while you're waiting for the trial. You may not think this has an awful lot to do with custody and visitation, but if you're living in a house owned by your co-parent with the children and he or she sells it out from under you, you will begin to think that it's very important. Likewise, one of these motions could be used to keep a savings account intact while you're waiting for the judge to divide it up or any of other personal property items like cars, motorcycles, or anything else.

Even after a temporary hearing, there can be many issues that were not considered in the drafting of the temporary order. For example, if your temporary hearing occurs in February, you may not be thinking about summer vacation or possibly even spring break. There might be a necessity in the meantime to go back to court and have the judge decide what sort of visitation will be appropriate for these times, if any. You can't assume that you will have a trial date close enough to your temporary hearing that these issues won't come up. They generally do come up because it takes so long in most jurisdictions and districts to get a trial date.

There can be emergency hearings that are necessary during the pendency of the trial. The emergency could be anything from a hearing to determine summer visitation (if it wasn't determined earlier in the temporary hearing) to a motion for additional visitation to allow the child to travel to a sick relative's bedside because the temporary order doesn't allow for that sort of thing. I've told you before the temporary orders should be as well thought out as is possible but no one can plan for every sort of emergency that might come up.

There can be modification hearings that come up while you're waiting for trial if the circumstances demand it. You may be forced to ask the judge for a different custody and visitation order because of events that happened during the course of your wait for the trial to occur. This would generate another temporary hearing. The sorts of events that may cause you to have a second temporary hearing would be those that change what you knew to be true at the time of the original temporary hearing. This sounds like it's getting involved but it's really not as difficult as all that.

Imagine for a moment that you are awarded temporary primary residential care with the children but six months into the temporary order, while you're waiting for the trial to happen, you are stopped and arrested for DUI with the children in the backseat. Your co-parent will probably ask for another temporary hearing to determine who is the better person to have primary residential care after that. Imagine another circumstance where your co-parent is awarded primary residential care of the children but suddenly he or she is deployed (in a military circumstance) outside of the country, or the job suddenly requires him or her to move 5000 miles away for a period of months or years. You would be the one asking the court for another temporary hearing. It's not difficult to understand how people's lives can change in an instant and what was a perfectly valid and understandable temporary hearing before the change can render the temporary custody order totally untenable and completely unworkable after. This is one of the really large problems with the overcrowding and the extremely long wait times in court these days.

MOTIONS FOR ORDERS OF CONTEMPT OR ENFORCEMENT

Sadly, these are the most often used or abused motions and hearings you will probably be involved with. The hearings on these issues are the result of motions filed in the court that are designed to make the judge aware of some action or inaction by one of the parties. Most often, the motion will state that the action or inaction that is complained of is in violation of some court order or possibly just the spirit of some court order.

The most common motion for order of contempt is known as the motion for order of civil contempt. Civil contempt is most often described as a violation of a court order or a failure to comply with a court order, away from the judge's presence, while the person still has the ability to comply or perform what's ordered by the court.

A person found in contempt of court is called a "contemnor." To prove contempt, the prosecutor or complainant must prove the four elements of contempt: existence of a lawful order, the potential contemnor's knowledge of the order, the potential contemnor's ability to comply, and the potential contemnor's failure to comply.

In the context of a custody and visitation scenario, the most often complained of violation of a court order is the one that deals with when, where, or how long the custody and visitation is to last. A motion for order of contempt may be filed under many circumstances with regard to custody and visitation. They most often occur regarding transfer of custody for the scheduled visitation or for transfer of custody back to the primary residential parent. I have seen motions for orders of contempt brought as a result of one parent or the other being as little as ten minutes late for the transfer. I have seen motions for contempt brought as a result of one parent or the other allowing a friend or family member to transport the child to the place where the transfers to occur. To be honest, I can't remember all of the ridiculous reasons why people filed motions for orders of contempt. In the last analysis, most of these motions could be dealt with by a simple phone call or realistic contact between the parents. For example, if your court order says that you are to exchange custody of the children at 6 p.m. on Sunday afternoons in a McDonald's parking lot and you are unable to get there at 6 p.m., a simple telephone call to inform the other parent that you will be there at 6:30 p.m. would cure most of the problems. Of course, if the lateness of the transfers is something that occurs weekly or the lateness is something that's intentional, it may be the subject of a motion for order of contempt after all.

The worst violations of custody and visitation orders occur when one parent just doesn't show up at all. This is not only impolite but is a clear violation of the custody or custody transfer order. You should not put yourself in a situation where you have to describe to a judge or explain to a judge why you did not appear at the appointed time and place to exchange custody of your child with your co-parent. Ninety-nine percent of the people in this country have a cell phone. The government even gives them away now to people who can't afford them. A judge is not going to believe that you had NO opportunity to call and inform anyone that you were not going to be there.

If a person is found in civil contempt, the judge has a number of different penalties that can be imposed for the contempt. If the contempt results in one parent losing time with the child, many states allow for makeup visitation by the child with the parent who lost the time. If the contempt caused one parent to lose money (such as loss of vacation plans, etc.) the judge may order the person causing the loss to pay for the loss in vacation time, reservations, or anything else. The harshest penalty would be that the judge actually changes the custody or visitation schedule so that the contempt may never happen again. Don't put yourself in this position. Judges remember which of you caused the problems when it comes down to the final hearing or trial.

The judge will always recall which party has been violating the court orders and will always hold it against that person. The final penalty for someone who violates a court order is that of attorney's fees. If you are found in contempt of court for a violation of a clear court order, the judge may, and often does, award your co-parent or spouse the costs associated with the drafting of a motion, the appearance in court, and the drafting of an order of contempt associated with your violation. Think about that. Not only do you have to pay your attorney for coming to court to defend you, you have to pay your co-parent's attorney because he or she had to come to court just to get you to comply with a court order.

A motion for enforcement of a court order is very similar to a motion for order of contempt in the custody and visitation setting. The motion is filed in order to get the judge to force the party who's not complying with the court order to change his or her conduct.

Motions for order of contempt and motions for enforcement can be brought for the smallest and simplest of violations all the way up to the largest violations. You have to be somewhat careful about filing these because if you continuously file motions for order of contempt because your co-parent is ten minutes late to drop off and pick up, you can be seen as a "pain in the neck" and a person who is not going to be cooperative with the nature and spirit of shared parental responsibility orders. We will all agree that a person who is routinely ten minutes late is a problem, but not so big a problem that you want to take up court time and end up with a case that costs a lot more than it should. Clear and substantive violations of court orders are completely different things. These are the matters that should be brought to the judge's attention in the form of motions for orders of contempt and motions for enforcement.

The "take away" on this is that you should never put yourself in a position that you can be found in contempt of court order. The "flipside" to this is you should not be bringing motions for orders of contempt against the co-parent if the violation of the court orders is so small that it makes you look silly because you brought it.

8

Mediation, Arbitration, and Alternative Dispute Resolution

There has been for approximately the last fifteen years a real push to get cases settled before they even reached the courthouse steps. I'm putting these three into one chapter because they all seem to qualify under the large heading of alternative dispute resolution processes.

COLLABORATIVE LAW

Collaborative law is loosely defined as *"a legal process enabling couples who have decided to separate or end their marriage to work with their lawyers and, on occasion, other family professionals in order to avoid the uncertain outcome of court and to achieve a settlement that best meets the specific needs of both parties and their children without the underlying threat of contested litigation. The voluntary process is initiated when the couple signs a contract (called the "participation agreement") binding each other to the process and disqualifying their respective lawyers' rights to represent either one in any future family related litigation. The collaborative process can be used to facilitate a broad range of other family issues, including disputes between parents and the drawing up of pre- and post-marital contracts. The traditional method of drawing up pre-marital contracts is oppositional, and many couples prefer to begin their married lives on a better footing where documents are drawn up consensually and together."*

There are certain benefits to collaborative law and certain drawbacks. The benefits are that both parties are prohibited from asking for court assistance during the collaboration process and thereby limiting the supposedly harmful effects of court hearings. Additionally, the collaborative process limits to a great degree the game playing and intimidation factors that usually go into a divorce or custody and visitation process.

The collaborative process forces people to negotiate with each other without the threat of court hearings and usually the discovery process is held to a minimum. The process presupposes that the parties have the ability and the willingness to work together to find solutions to their problems, including custody and visitation, and they are limited to utilization of attorneys only for purely legal advice during the process. Both parties and both attorneys must agree to the rules concerning collaborative law. It is supposed that this process can keep much if not all of the animosity, anger, and argument out of the process. If the process is successful, the two lawyers get an understanding of the agreement from the parties and a formal document of the agreement is drafted that would ultimately be given to the judge. The judge would adopt the agreement into a final judgment that would be entered into the record of the divorce or custody proceeding as a final resolution. The terms and conditions of the final judgment (which adopts the agreement of the parties) would then be as enforceable as if there had been a trial on the matter and a decision was made by the court.

Sounds great, right?

The downside is that if the collaborative law process does not work, you have wasted a lot of time, money, and options in the attempt. One or the other of you will be really angry (or maybe both) because of all the time wasted and the money spent only to have to start completely over. It's almost like a double or nothing bet. Either it works, and you end up happy (or as happy as you can be after the breakup) or doesn't work, and you have wasted everything up to that moment. Also if the process does not work, you cannot use the lawyer you chose for the collaborative process to be your lawyer after that. So, if you read *Divorce and Conquer* and found the best lawyer you could find in your area, you are now prohibited from using that lawyer by the agreement you entered into.

I investigated collaborative law at one point in time during my practice. I made a decision that it was not for me. I have told you before that my relationship with my clients became very personal and it would be very difficult for me to be prohibited from representing them to the best of my ability and skill after a negotiating process like that had failed. My friends who engaged in collaborative law told me that their experience was about fifty percent successful. Of course, this means that fifty percent of the collaborative law cases they engaged and were unsuccessful.

In some markets there are law firms that do nothing but collaborative law. This means they do not go to court or have never been to court. Think about that.

MEDIATION

Mediation is a process that has a good and successful history. The process itself is described as *"a form of alternative dispute resolution (ADR), a way of resolving disputes between two or more parties with concrete effects. Typically, a third party, the mediator, assists the parties to negotiate a settlement. Disputants may mediate disputes in a variety of domains, such as commercial, legal, diplomatic, workplace, community and family matters.*

The term "mediation" broadly refers to any instance in which a third party helps others reach agreement. More specifically, mediation has a structure, timetable and dynamics that "ordinary" negotiation lacks. The process is private and confidential, possibly enforced by law. Participation is typically voluntary. The mediator acts as a neutral third party and facilitates rather than directs the process."

For approximately the last fifteen years mediation has been an integral part of the family law litigation process. Most judges will require the parties to a divorce or a custody and visitation issue to attend one or more mediations before they can apply for final court time or trial.

The discovery process may or may not be complete when the mediation happens. Most good lawyers will insist that all "discovery" is complete, however, before they engage in a final mediation. This means that a temporary mediation can occur before a temporary hearing and another or final mediation can occur before the final hearing or the trial. Mediations with regard to custody and visitation are extremely popular among the judges as well as the Family Law Bar Association because they can be successful in so many situations without wasting too much time or money.

Mediations can have one of three different outcomes. (1) The mediation can be completely successful, at which point the mediator or one of the attorneys will draft up an agreement which will be presented to the judge and will almost always form the basis of a final judgment. (2) The mediation can be partially successful, at which point the mediator or one of the attorneys will draft up a partial agreement to be presented to the judge and will undoubtedly form the basis of a partial final judgment. (3) The mediation is not successful, at which point the mediator will send to the judge what's known as "a notice of impasse" and the case will be put back in the ordinary trial stance. When a notice of impasse is sent to the judge, there is no assignment of guilt or innocence and the judge has no way of knowing why the case wouldn't settle. The only thing that the judge knows when he or she receives the notice of impasse is that the parties had been to mediation and had tried but were unable to settle. There is no penalty assigned to parties who are unable to mediate or settle their matter. I will tell you, however, that when the case does go to trial, usually the judge can tell which one of the parties was at fault for the failure of the mediation just by the way the trial goes. If one party is unreasonable and asks for things that are silly, it's not difficult to figure out.

In my practice, mediations were completely successful about forty percent of the time. This meant that all litigation and legal hostilities ceased as far as the mediated issue went and within a matter of days or weeks, the parties began to live under the agreement they had reached and had been adopted by the judge and a court order. In approximately another twenty percent of the time the mediation was partially successful, which meant that the parties were able to agree on some aspects, but not all, of their case. Even in the cases where the parties were only partially successful, the degree of animosity and polarization generally lessened. The fact that some of the case had been settled gave both parties a degree of confidence and satisfaction that was not there before the mediation. In about forty percent of the cases, the parties were unable to come to any kind of agreement, either partial or full, and the case went back into a litigation posture as though no attempt had ever been made to settle it.

The mediation process can be started by either the agreement of the parties or their lawyers, or an order by the court can be issued to attend mediation. I told you before that in most jurisdictions currently, the Family Court process includes at least one and sometimes two mediations before the parties can schedule a trial.

The first thing that has to happen will be the agreement or the assignment of a mediator. In some jurisdictions, the mediation process is part of the court system itself and parties are assigned to a mediator within that department. In some jurisdictions, the parties can choose either the "court" mediator or agree on a mediator of their own. These are called private mediators. Generally, the benefit to a private mediator is the degree of expertise that the mediator has in the problem that is going to be discussed. If your case, for example, goes to a "court mediator," that person could have a great deal of experience possibly in financial matters or support cases but might not have any experience whatsoever in custody and visitation matters. My experience was always that it was better to pick the mediator rather than have one assigned. That way your attorney and the other attorney can agree on using a lawyer or psychologist who has a great deal of experience in custody and visitation matters and can understand the problems presented as a result of all that experience.

The mediation must be scheduled for a time and place that is convenient for you, your co-parent, both of your lawyers and the mediator. It is preferable to have the mediation in the conference room of the mediator's office. That way nobody has a sense of "home turf."

The mediator will usually require payment for a minimum number of hours before the mediation commences. (I always required four hours in advance.) There can be a great deal of difference in the amount of money you will spend on a mediator based on the level of experience he or she may have. The "court" mediators usually have a strict schedule of costs and fees they charge but are routinely much cheaper than private mediators. A private mediator can charge whatever he or she wants to and it's always about the same amount they charge per hour in their practice. I experienced mediation fees ranging from $150 per hour to $400 per hour. In law, as in mediators, the adage works. You get what you pay for. Paying a mediator for an afternoon may be the best money you ever spent. Would you rather pay for an inexpensive mediator and get a poor or no result, or spend the extra money on a chance to finish the matter today? My advice is to authorize your lawyer to use the mediator who has a lot of experience and works well with both your lawyer and the other lawyer involved.

The mediation process itself will start with all of you in the same room. There is only one exception to this rule and that is in cases where there may have been physical or spousal violence in the past. If one party asks the mediator to exclude the other party as a result of some fear or intimidation, the mediator will respect that request. In that case the mediator will both start and finish with the parties in different rooms and never bring them together. At the beginning, if everyone is together, the mediator will probably give a small speech about the process and how it works. All mediators are taught to begin the process in a similar way. Both of you will be told to be courteous and not interrupt when the other is speaking. You will be asked to confirm your commitment to the mediation process which means you will try to negotiate all matters in good faith and not to cause any more anger or polarization.

The mediator will then probably ask the moving party (the plaintiff or petitioner) to give a brief statement of what the issues are. The mediator might ask at the end of that statement what the petitioner proposes as far as a resolution of the issues. The mediator will ask either you or your attorney to give the statement. There is no set rule on whether you should do it or whether your attorney should do it. It is something that you should have discussed with your attorney before you get there; and if you are going to be the one to give the opening statement, it should have been something that you had practiced in your attorney's office before starting. The statement should be clear and give causes or reasons for your issues. You should not go into too much detail as far as this opening statement goes but save it for a discussion with the mediator in private. After you are finished with your opening statement, the mediator will ask your ex or co-parent for his or her version of the facts and the suggested resolution. Just because you are the one who gives the opening statement, you shouldn't be surprised if your ex's lawyer gives the opening statement for him or her.

After the opening statement, a mediator will probably divide you up so that you and your lawyer are in one room and your ex and his or her lawyer are in another room. This process is called "caucusing." The mediator then makes a decision as to which of the two rooms he or she will visit first. This is completely up to the mediator. I was a mediator myself for many years and my practice was to go to the room of the petitioner first, following the order that was established with the opening statements. As I said before, however, this is completely up to the mediator and yours may do something different. I know there are mediators who will move to the "problem" room first to try to soften their position. When I say there is a "problem" room, I mean that possibly the mediator can tell which of you is going to be more of a problem in the mediation process. Sometimes people have a problem with the mediation process simply because they are nervous or have anxiety about what's happening. In that case, the mediator can help with those fears and possibly calm that person down in order to bring him or her back to a reasonable position. Otherwise, the "problem" can be the one who is acting unreasonably or has taken a position that's unreasonable.

In the caucusing stage of the mediation, you will be able to tell the mediator what you're thinking and what is happened without the information being transmitted to the other party. Mediators are required to keep secret what they hear in the "caucus" phase unless or until they have been released by the party who said it to tell the other person. You can be as open and honest as you want to be during this caucusing part of the process. This is the place where the mediator "picks up" on where your priorities and your needs are regarding the problem. In a situation of custody and visitation, the mediator absolutely needs to know your priorities and where you are and are not willing to negotiate. Of course, if both parties are determined to be "the primary residential parent" and are completely unwilling to negotiate that issue, many times the mediation will simply fail. I found, however, that during the caucusing part of the process many people were willing to negotiate with me as a mediator something they were not willing to negotiate with their ex. As the mediator, I was then able to go to the other parent and find out what his or her priorities were. I then fashioned the basis of an agreement and tried to lead both parties into that agreement.

The caucusing phase can take minutes or hours. It's up to you and the mediator to determine which it will be. The mediator may try to bring all parties back into the same room at different times during the caucusing phase in order to get agreements on small or inconsequential bits of a developing custody and visitation agreement. The theory is that each agreement is made up of small bits and pieces, and if you can agree on all of the small parts, then you can agree on the big picture. In other words, the mediator is trying to get you to agree on small pieces of a larger agreement so that you will feel "vested" in the process. This is a common negotiating practice.

Sooner or later, the mediator will bring all parties and the attorneys back into the same room. The mediator will then attempt to fashion a full or partial agreement for everybody to sign before the parties leave. It may be that no agreement is possible and this final meeting among all the parties will be when the mediator tells everyone that he or she is not going to be able to help them. The mediator will do one of two things at that point. He or she will either draft a full or partial agreement for everyone to sign or will inform everyone that an "impasse" has been reached, and he or she is of the opinion that further mediation is impossible or will not lead to any results. At that point the mediation will be over.

There are certified mediators and uncertified mediators. Certified mediators have not only been to the mediation course which is generally forty hours but they have observed a set number of mediations in order to qualify for the certification process.

Certified mediators operate under a set of rules which include a prohibition on their interjecting anything of their personality or expertise in the process. This means they're not supposed to give an opinion on the strength or weakness of a position, or chances in court to anyone. Uncertified mediators are not constrained like that and may give an option for some people. There can be a situation where a strong and opinionated mediator can be just what a case needs to get it moving. You'll have to talk to your attorney and see what he or she feels would be the best for your case.

I have spent a lot of time on mediations because they are a really important moment in your lawsuit. I always describe it to clients as their "last, best chance to settle it themselves." I believed it then and I believe it now. A resolution that is fashioned by the parties is much more likely to be enforceable and is much more likely to be adhered to by the parties rather than one fashioned by a judge that nobody's going to be completely happy with.

PARENTING COORDINATORS

Parenting Coordinators are described as being a relatively new practice used in some states to manage ongoing issues in high-conflict child custody and visitation cases by a professional psychologist or a lawyer assigned by the Court. There are ten states as of May 2011 that have passed legislation regarding Parenting Coordinators: Colorado (since 2005), Idaho (2002), Louisiana (2007), New Hampshire (2009), North Carolina

(2005), Oklahoma (2001), Oregon (2002), Texas (2005), and Massachusetts and Florida (2009). Parenting Coordinators are usually of two types: licensed professionals in a mental health or pastoral field of counseling, or they are attorneys who are in good standing with their state's Bar Association. There may be more states now that are unreported.

I'll be honest with you here. I have a kind of a love/hate relationship with Parenting Coordinators. They can be a great tool in the lawyer's or the court's arsenal of weapons with which to solve conflicts. However, some are just "officious inter-meddlers" that seem to magnify some problems. Additionally if the parties get addicted to taking their problems to a parenting coordinator, it can be a never-ending type of therapy that doesn't cure the problem. The shrewd or clever custodial parent can use the Parenting Coordinator to draw out the time of their custody over the children and stall the transfer of custody utilizing small or insignificant problems. For example, I've seen situations where a custodial parent will refuse to give over the children for visitation with a noncustodial parent UNTIL there has been a meeting between both of the parties and the Parenting Coordinator to work out some problem. Ordinarily the problem is not anything serious but may be something truly mundane that ordinary parents should be able to work out among themselves. Again, one party or the other can become addicted to the process and will learn that the benefit of the delay of the process and getting a second opinion on a disputed issue can draw out, at best, or completely defeat, at worst, the learning process when it comes to the parties being able to solve their own problems. The "Coordinator" is all the while charging hundreds of dollars an hour for the service which rapidly becomes an incurable habit.

The Parenting Coordinator has wide ranging powers, once appointed, including but not necessarily limited to:

The Parenting Coordinator can limit where parents can and cannot go during his/her daily routine with the child, and what activities are allowed.

The Parenting Coordinator can prevent parents from discussing certain topics with their children in their conversations.

The Parenting Coordinator can take complaints from either party about almost any subject of the other party's conduct during the past visit, and make decisions the parties must abide with. For example, the PC can decide what sports kids will attend, what friends they can visit, what religious services to attend, what food parents can feed them and more.

The Parenting Coordinator can make decisions in cases when the parties do not agree on child non-urgent medical care.

The Parenting Coordinator can decide when, where, and how the non-custodial parent's family and friends are allowed to see the children.

The Parenting Coordinator can report suspected child abuse to Child Protective Services.

and many more of what can be considered as "child best interests."

If either party does not agree with the PC (as they're sometimes called) recommendations, then he or she can file a motion with the court to make a decision on the disputed issue. Either party can also ask the court to appoint a new PC to the case but has to provide sufficient evidences to convince the court that valid reasons exist.

You can tell just from this list that the Parenting Coordinator has a *tremendous* degree of control over your life and the lives of your children while you are under court order to undergo this process.

Don't get me wrong, most of these people are truly interested in helping you and guiding you through the process. However, you must make sure that you don't fall into the trap of relying on them too much for day-to-day decisions. You also have to make the Parenting Coordinator aware if you believe that your co-parent is falling into the trap.

You notice that the last sentence where I was describing the Parenting Coordinator's powers says that "either party can also ask the court to appoint a new PC to the case but has to provide sufficient evidence to convince the court that valid reasons exist." This means that you have to have a convincing reason, other than your dissatisfaction with some ruling that the PC has made, and you'll have to wait until you have a hearing date in order to make that change and only if the judge agrees with you. It could take months to get that hearing and you will probably be under the control of the very Parenting Coordinator you're complaining about the whole time.

If the Court is inclined to appoint a Parenting Coordinator in your case, my best result has been to have your attorney insist on a limited number of meetings or weeks that you are required to engage in the process. My belief is that a Parenting Coordinator who knows their power is only for a limited duration will feel the pressure to complete the task and will undertake to get you both on the right track as soon as possible. An open-ended court order without a termination date just gives the Parenting Coordinator too much power, and it is too tempting to rely on them for too long. After all, visitation is a thing that should be agreed upon by both parents and you should be able to work it out. The Parenting Coordinator should be a person who gives you tips or guidance, not be a referee between the two of you for the rest of your lives. The more trips you make to the Parenting Coordinator, the more the rules can mount up and the smaller the rules can become. Before long, you'll have to carry the "rules" around with you on a piece of paper to remember them all.

There have been arguments made in various states concerning the powers awarded to Parenting Coordinators as being unconstitutional in that they violate the 4th and 14th amendments concerning due process, etc. The basis of the concerns are that Parenting Coordinators are exercising powers reserved only for judges and only after a hearing where both sides have an opportunity to be heard. A Parenting Coordinator is not really an officer of the court but a sort of consultant. This seems to give "judge type" powers to someone who's not a judge, doesn't it? Personally, I think these are valid arguments because they do deprive people of a right that they have without due process of law. The real problem, however, is that the unscrupulous Parenting Coordinator or co-parent can draw the process out and simply create a situation where they become the unbridled referee or judge between parents for much too long of a time.

You will have to have a conversation with your lawyer if you think this issue is going to come up to find out about your judge's thoughts on the subject. If you have a judge who uses them a lot, you may have no option but to go through it. Your only real opportunity at that point will be just to insist on a limited duration. If you have a judge who doesn't do it very often or will only do it by agreement of the parties, your lawyer will have to give you his or her opinion on the Parenting Coordinators who are available in your area and whether or not he or she has had success with them.

Remember, Parenting Coordinators come with their own sets of prejudices and are not policed by appellate courts. If they are the types who don't like kids playing football, hockey, boxing, or anything else, you may have a rough time if you want those sports in your child's life.

Another thing. They can always be called to testify in a hearing and may in fact volunteer sometimes. You have NO expectation of privacy with a Parenting Coordinator like you had with the mediator, so you should ALWAYS be careful what you say in front of him or her.

TAKEAWAYS

There may be more than these alternative dispute resolution vehicles in your circuit or district. As you can tell, some of them may work for you and some may not. It will always be a subject that you can have a conversation with your attorney about and you absolutely should. Each comes with its own set of benefits and drawbacks.

9

Psychologists, Psychiatrists, Guardians Ad Litem and Custody Evaluators

I have lumped these professionals into one chapter, but they can be called on to do many different types of tasks. They are, however, all professional witnesses in that they conduct an evaluation and they give a professional opinion in court or can testify about their thoughts on the family dynamic.

The bad news. Some of them are not very good and some of them just do it for the money. You're going to have to take your lawyer's advice on which of these people you should hire and which you should stay away from. If you're like me, your entire life you always considered psychologists, psychiatrists and people who performed custody evaluations to be of sterling character and would never ever slant their testimony one way or the other simply because they were being paid by one person or the other to do it. You may have been wrong about that.

One of the things you'll have to do is to try to find out how many times one of these witnesses has testified on behalf of your lawyer or on behalf of your co-parent's lawyer. If your co-parent's lawyer has used only one psychologist, psychiatrist, or custody evaluator for the last twenty years and has routinely received helpful testimony in court and good evaluations, you will probably want to stay away from that witness. How do you find this out? You ask both of them in a deposition or in interrogatories. You can force the witness and the lawyer to divulge how many times the witness has testified on behalf of that lawyer and how many times the evaluation has been favorable to that lawyer's client. You can also ask both the lawyer and the witness if they have a personal relationship as in dating, playing golf together, or any other definition of a personal relationship.

The really bad news. They cost a fortune. They can charge anywhere from $200 an hour to $500 an hour for their analysis, investigation, and written evaluations. They can charge more than that if they have to come to court and testify. It can get so expensive that you won't believe it.

The good news. Most of them are ethical, thoughtful, and do the right thing every single day of their lives. If you are fortunate enough to have the kind of money it takes to employ one of these people to testify in your case, he or she can be the most powerful evidence and provide the most convincing testimony of any witness that you can call.

PSYCHOLOGISTS AND PSYCHIATRISTS

Both psychologists and psychiatrists can be custody evaluators, but for this section we are going to deal with them as just witnesses with regard to the mental or emotional state of your co-parent, you, your children, and possibly any other people who live in your home or who will have day-to-day access or contact with the children.

Both psychologists and psychiatrists have exhaustive training in mental and emotional problems and their therapies. A psychiatrist is also an M.D. A psychologist (at this level) has a doctorate in psychology and a significant amount of clinical training as well. For the most part, both psychologists and psychiatrists will narrow their fields so that they become experts in whatever pursuit that might be. Some of them narrow it to the extent that they become expert in child psychology or psychiatry and they are really good at their jobs.

You can find out if the person being recommended to conduct an analysis or evaluation on you or any family member has a specialty by asking for their curriculum vitae, or CV for short. The curriculum vitae will tell you where the person went to school and what degrees were received. It will generally tell you of any honors for any extracurricular activities that person engaged in also. The CV will tell you about any clinical studies or outside clinical work the person has been involved with and any post graduate work the person has done. You will be able to tell ordinarily just from the CV if this is a person you want doing the evaluation or analysis. How do you get this information? If your lawyer has been working with this person in the past, he or she will probably have a copy of the CV in their office. If your lawyer hasn't worked with this person in the past or this is a person who is being proposed by the other side, you will be able to get a copy of it simply by asking, or in discovery if it's necessary.

Why do we need one of these? There are many reasons. If you suspect your spouse or co-parent is or is becoming emotionally unbalanced or could possibly become a problem for the children, you would want him or her to be evaluated by someone. A psychologist or psychiatrist can either tell you that it's not true or come to court and tell the judge that it is true and make the information available to the court. If you know or suspect that your ex has become addicted to drugs, you may want to have him or her evaluated for that so that the psychiatrist or psychologist can testify what effects that drug addiction can have on the children. There are people who are addiction specialists and specialize in the finding and treatment of addictions. If your ex has a crazy father, brother, or uncle who routinely visits, you may want to have that person analyzed and evaluated before your custody and visitation matter is concluded so that you can either be confident about their closeness to the children or make sure that that closeness doesn't turn into something bad.

You may want to have one or more of the children evaluated (aside from the custody evaluation) for any signs that they may show or be showing about the breakup or anything else that's worrisome for you before the trial. You may even suspect parental alienation. Then that witness can come in and testify about recommendations or proposals to help the child.

The options for utilization of one of these witnesses, as you can probably tell, are endless. You're really going to need to talk to your lawyer about it, though, because not only the expense but the effect on the child and your relationship with your ex may be harmed or altered. If there's even a chance that it may look to the judge like you're reaching for evidence that's not there or you're trying to manufacture some problem, you'll want to forget it. Using a psychologist or psychiatrist can backfire on you and can turn out to be catastrophic to your case. Be careful.

How do you get one? I've never known any ex or co-parent to voluntarily submit to a psychological or psychiatric evaluation. Your lawyer will probably ask first but in reality, in order to get a psychological or psychiatric evaluation done on your ex or any one of the children, you'll probably have to make a motion before the court and get a court order. The psychological or psychiatric evaluation will probably have to be limited in scope to just the issues you're worried or complain about. Obviously, if the psychologist or the psychiatrist finds something else that may be worrisome, he or she will bring it to your lawyer's attention and ultimately to the judge's attention. So, in addition to the expense of the psychologist or psychiatrist, you will have the added expense of having to pay your lawyer to draft up the motion and attend the hearing. I can assure you that your ex won't submit to something like this quietly. It could happen, but I doubt it.

GUARDIANS AD LITEM

A guardian ad litem is a guardian appointed by a court to protect the interests of a minor or incompetent in a particular matter. The *ad litem* part is a Latin phrase which roughly translates to mean "for legal purposes."

State law and local court rules govern the appointment of guardians ad litem. Typically, the court may appoint either a lawyer or a court appointed special volunteer to serve as guardian ad litem in juvenile matters, family court matters, probate matters, and domestic relations matters. The guardian ad litem is not expected to make diagnostic or therapeutic recommendations but is expected to provide an information base from which to draw resources. As authorized by law, the guardian ad litem may present evidence and ensure that, where appropriate, witnesses are called and examined, including, but not limited to, foster parents and psychiatric, psychological, medical, or other expert witnesses. (US Legal.com)

The above is the typically accepted definition of a guardian ad litem in most states that provide for their utilization. Sometimes if a judge is getting conflicting reports or recommendations either from the parents or in some cases from other witnesses, he or she may want to appoint a guardian ad litem. I have known guardians ad litem who are masters level psychologists also. The thinking is that the best guardian ad litem would be a lawyer so that if there was any legal action to be taken on the child's behalf, the lawyer could do it quickly and effectively without going back to the court to get permission. If a guardian ad litem suspects child or spousal abuse, or parental alienation as a result of the interviews with the child, the guardian ad litem can inform the court or take steps to see that it's investigated and dealt with.

Crafty and cunning lawyers will utilize the guardian ad litem to testify about what a child wants or needs without having the child come to court and actually give the testimony themselves. I have told you before that most judges do not want a child testifying in court at all. This could be a way that the child's testimony could come in to the record through the guardian ad litem without violating that prohibition. For example, it would be a sneaky and effective way to get the child's preference on where she or he wanted to live (and with whom) and never get on the wrong side of the judge.

Guardians ad litem can be either paid or volunteers. You'll have to ask your attorney what the normal situation is in your circuit or district. The vast majority I have known are volunteers and do the work simply because they feel the need to help the children involved in a custody fight in some way. If you feel as though your child might not be truthful for some reason or might be concealing something that may be embarrassing to him or her, you may want to consider the guardian ad litem. If you feel as though your child is concealing something about your ex because of the embarrassment or problems it may cause your ex, this may be an option for you to have the child "get it out" without him or her having to go through a psychological or psychiatric exam.

My experience is that guardians ad litem are extremely valuable tools and can be good for not only the case but also for the children.

How do you get one? This is sometimes easier to get than a psychologist or psychiatrist. In many cases, both spouses can agree on the benefit of a guardian ad litem. If one spouse has something to hide or something they really don't want brought out in court, that spouse may resist the idea of a guardian ad litem. Generally, all you have to do is ask, but if your ex is resistive, you can make a motion before the court. Usually the motion doesn't have to contain an awful lot of complaints or allegations. You may have to voice some suspicions, however, such as the child is being secretive or doesn't want to talk about a particular subject. If the guardian ad litem program in your area consists of volunteers, there won't be any expense. If they are not volunteers, you may be responsible for the expense if you're the one asking.

CUSTODY EVALUATORS

Custody evaluators are professionals who give testimony concerning a wide range of family dynamics. They can be utilized to evaluate and analyze the relationships of parents with their children, parents with each other, and siblings with each other. The custody evaluation is the most widely utilized psychological or psychiatric tool in the lawyer's arsenal to give the judge a professional look at what's going on within your family. They will (or at least should) always be a PhD. psychologist or a psychiatrist.

A custody evaluation is an extremely invasive and sometimes painful process to go through. You should talk to your lawyer about it before you get involved in it.

Procedurally, the evaluation will involve a number of different interviews with the psychologist or psychiatrist who is assigned or ordered to do it. These interviews will be of you alone and also of you with the children. The evaluator may ask that you also be interviewed with your spouse or co-parent. If the evaluator is a psychologist, there will probably be some written tests such as the Minnesota Multiphasic or possibly some other personality evaluating multiple-choice test. These tests will probably be given to both you and your co-parent or anyone else acting as a parent in your children's lives. The tests will usually come first, and the interviews will come after the tests have been scored and evaluated. The tests are to give the psychologist data with regard to your particular personality traits and what he or she should expect from you.

The interviews will consist of question-and-answer as well as observation. **You will probably be observed in the evaluator's waiting room while waiting to get in to the interview.** The observation will be to see how you interact with the child when you think no one is watching. I have known evaluators to put a great deal of stock in just these ten minute observations before the interviews actually start. If you are observed to be interactive with the child, on a play level, as well as possibly reading to the child during this time, it will go a long way toward setting up the tone of the interview when you do get into the presence of the evaluator. If you are observed in the waiting room ignoring the child or reading a magazine, believe me, it will show up in the evaluation. The interviews with the children will generally contain some sort of interaction observation as well. You may be assigned some tasks to perform with the child that involves both of your participation. The success or failure of the task is not terribly important; it is the degree of your participation and cooperation that is being graded. If your child is an adolescent or teenager, the observation will be about how you deal with their problems and how you react to what they have the say. You should not be confrontational during these meetings. It's a fine line, I know, but you have to be in charge while not being overbearing. The evaluator is going to want to see your parenting skills. Make sure that he or she sees them. You just can't lose your temper and you can't be too forceful. Remember, these people are psychologists and psychiatrists. For the most part, they want everybody to be happy and negotiating. If you're too forceful, you can be making a mistake.

Above all, you should appear to be happy to engage in this process and get it across to the evaluator that your only concern is for the child(ren) and you want to be a better parent when this is over. This may be the place where you impress the evaluator with the books you have read on the subject of single parenting or dealing with your ex after divorce.

Above all, you have to be engaged. For example, if you have been an absentee father during the course of your marriage or relationship but you have an infant you're trying to get overnight custody with or extended visitation for the summer, you have to be able to change the child's diaper. Don't just say you're going learn how to do it; you have to be able to do it with a smile on your face, while carrying on a conversation with the evaluator and not throw up or turn green. Also in that vein, you should think of what you should have before you get to the evaluation. You should not be borrowing your ex's car seat. You should have one of your own. You should have a bag with diapers, baby wipes, oil, and all of the other items that a person who has a baby should have with him or her. Your ex has told the evaluator that you are completely unprepared to be left alone with this infant for more than an hour or two. Believe me, if you show up to the evaluation with a full diaper bag and you can change a diaper, clean the baby, and carry on a conversation without throwing up, you will have convinced the evaluator that you're okay and you probably won't have anything else to prove, assuming you're not drunk.

These things you have to think about should be those that have already been done for the first time before you go to this evaluation. Generally, people who have recently separated take months to get their new apartment ready for the kids to come over even though they want the kids to come over the first week after the separation. If you're the one who moved out of the house, you should already have a bed, sheets, towels, and some of the child or children's possessions in your new place before the kids even get there. Certainly it should all be set up by the time you meet with the evaluator the first time. You may want to take some pictures with you of the child's room in your new place.

Some of these things are according to the child's age is well. I have never known a stay-at-home mother of a toddler to go out of the house without a bag full of children's toys, a Zip-lock full of Cheerios, and something for the child to drink. This comes from experience. When you go to see the evaluator, you should have your own bag of toys, and books, and handy wipes, and anything else you think you might need while you're out for the afternoon with a child. If you don't know what these are, find out. Call your sister or your mother and find out what should be in that bag. If you're the parent of an adolescent, there could be a problem. Adolescents and teenagers have electronic devices they are really attached to. You're going to have to separate the kids from those devices somehow and get them to engage with you for a while. If you can get them off the phone, the game device (or whatever) for an hour while you're at the evaluator's office, you're going to impress that evaluator just by the fact that you're able to do it.

You're going have to be able to do these things in a way that shows the evaluator that you're confident about it and you're happy doing it.

Sounds like a lot of work and preparation doesn't it? Well, it **is** a lot of work and preparation. I told you in the first chapter that preparation is everything in this ordeal. If you have never changed a diaper you're going to have to learn, and you're going to have to prove it to someone. If you have never dealt with a petulant three-year-old, you're going to have to learn how to do that, too. But all of these things are going to have to be obvious to the evaluator the first time you walk through the door because you may never get a second chance to prove yourself on any of this stuff. I would love to be able to tell you how to get an adolescent or teenager to engage civilly with their parents, but that's something I haven't figured out yet either. Sorry.

If there is something in your ex's history that needs to be brought out, this will be the point to do it. If he or she has been treated for depression, mental illness of some sort, bipolar or borderline personality issues, now is the time to talk about it. Likewise, if you're ex has been involved in criminal activity that they were convicted of and you think it may have some impact on their ability to parent on their own or deal with you in the future, this is the time to bring that up as well. Even if your ex has a conviction for something unrelated to his or her ability to deal with you or your child(ren), you should mention it but not dwell on it. There will probably be a moment in these interviews that the evaluator will ask you about your ex's past and anything that you need to bring up to give the evaluator and accurate and adequate picture of who your ex really is. You should assume your ex will be happy to enlighten the evaluator about any problems you've had with regard to emotional issues, addictions, and criminal history also. I wouldn't rely on this too heavily. If the evaluator feels like the information you're giving is relevant and important, he or she will either ask you more questions about it (the years, treatment, etc.) or will simply look into it personally and ask your ex. A child abuse case against your ex last year is going to be a lot more interesting to the evaluator than when he or she stole a car twenty-five years ago. See what I mean?

The evaluator will probably ask you at some point to give him or her names and phone numbers of some people you would like for them to talk to. These will be people who will be able to assure the evaluator that you are who you appear to be and that you are safe with the kids either on a primary custody basis or on an extended visitation basis. Think about who these people are going to be before you get there. Everyone gives their mom as the first name on the list. It's okay; you're expected to do it. The other four or five names, however, should be people you know will verify everything you told the evaluator. If you have told the evaluator you are the person who is involved with the Little League football program, then you should have the name and phone number of your kid's coach (and he should recognize your name). If you have told the evaluator that you're the person who looks after the child's medical needs, you should have the name and phone number of the nurse in the doctor's office who makes the appointments. If one of the names is going to be your ex's parole officer, call him first and get him ready for the call.

You should be reviewing all of the considerations contained in Chapter 5 of this book before you see the evaluator. The evaluator is aware of these criteria and will be looking for indicators in what you say to correlate to those. You should not focus on the legalistic criteria too much, though. Remember who you're dealing with. Psychiatrists and psychologists are going to be looking more into the "touchy-feely" parts of the criteria. Issues like your love for the child, the child's love for you, moral fitness, sexual or domestic violence are going to be what will "push their buttons." You should express your feelings that your child should have a rich and on-going relationship with the other parent and your willingness to champion and encourage that relationship. You should maybe ask the evaluator to help you think of ways to encourage that relationship. After all, these evaluators are practitioners most of the time. They LOVE to tell people how to act and how to make themselves better people emotionally and mentally. You could show or tell the evaluator about your parenting plan during these meetings and even engage the evaluator in the small or final parts of the plan. Asking for and getting advice from the evaluator on the finishing touches of the plan may get the evaluator "on board" with you in your efforts to get custody or extended visitation.

This process will, of necessity, involve a great deal of searching within yourself. In order to change that *future* history you will need to be able to admit past mistakes and to already have a plan in place to make sure you don't make those mistakes again. Your plan for avoiding mistakes must be something that comes out of your mouth as easily as reciting your address or phone number. What I'm telling you here is that you can't just "talk the talk" and get away with it. You must be able to "walk the walk." If these evaluators feel like they're being manipulated, it will not be a good day for you and all this preparation will be for nothing.

There will come a time when the evaluator is finished with the evaluation. All of the interviews will have been conducted, the testing and the scoring will have been calculated, and he or she will set about the task of writing up his or her evaluation for presentation to the attorneys. By this point, all of your preparation has been done and you have taken the tests, gone to the meetings, and done everything you can do to make the evaluator believe that you are who you say you are.

The evaluators are human beings. They can miss things. If there is something in the evaluation that was taken wrong or was missed by the evaluator, you can tell your attorney about it and he or she can ask the evaluator about it during a deposition. For example, if you have discussed your parenting plan with the evaluator but he or she has forgotten about it or it's not reflected in their notes, you can bring it up in the form of questions either in a deposition or in the trial. You have to be careful about this, though, because most of these evaluators have pretty big egos and may become defensive if an error or a lapse is brought to their attention.

A well thought out and investigated child custody evaluation is probably the best tool that lawyers have to negotiating a settlement. A child custody evaluation that goes against you, while difficult to overcome, is not the catastrophe you might think. A good trial lawyer may be able to cross-examine a child custody evaluator out of a position or two and actually have the testimony by the evaluator discounted by the judge because they are not certain on those few things or are just not strong enough to back up their recommendations. Additionally, some recommendations can be changed during the course of the trial based on testimony the evaluator hears in the trial. Remember, some professional witnesses, like child custody evaluators, are allowed to come to court and listen to the testimony of the witnesses if it helps them make their decision.

10

The Trial: What Will It Be Like and What Should You Expect?

BEFORE THE TRIAL ACTUALLY STARTS

You've been through all of the discovery processes, the evaluations, and all of the preliminary hearings. So, all that's left is the trial. Let's go through it.

A trial is generally scheduled by the judge who will be presiding over it. Each individual judge has his or her own way of scheduling trials. Some allow the attorneys to just ask for trial time and reserve the time on the judge's calendar. Some judges require what's called a status conference. We touched on the status conference briefly in some of the earlier chapters. A status conference can be either requested by one or both of the attorneys or the judge can simply set it on his or her own motion. A status conference is generally of very short duration and covers very limited topics.

The status conference for the purpose of setting a trial usually comes with a notice of hearing to both you and your attorney that requires you to do certain things. In some jurisdictions you have to certify or provide proof that you have attended a "parenting course" and possibly some other courses, depending on your jurisdiction. Your attorney may have to provide a document stating that all discovery or investigation is completed and there are no pending motions or problems affecting the scheduling of the trial. In some jurisdictions, the attorneys have to provide a statement as to their estimate of the length of time necessary for the trial. They may also have to provide a final list of possible witnesses and also a schedule or list of evidence or possible evidence that they will be using during the trial. The list of possible witnesses and the list of possible evidence may be necessary in order to avoid arguments during the assigned trial time. Evidence that a witness may give or possibly the admissibility of the evidence that your lawyer may be trying to get into the record or that the other attorney is trying to get into the record may be the cause of an evidentiary argument that takes up time.

The rules of evidence provide that any document to be produced in evidence requires a person to authenticate it before it can be used. In some jurisdictions it is possible to waive "authentication" if the parties agree that the evidence is authentic. This can relieve both parties of the necessity of having witnesses come to court and simply point to a document and say "Yes, that's mine" or possibly "Yes, that is a business record of mine." It's not unusual for this to be done.

Most of the time, the status conference will be the moment that the trial is actually scheduled. You and your lawyer, your ex and his or her lawyer, and the judge should all have their day books or calendars available so that the scheduling can be written into the judge's calendar and everybody else's as well. A certain date (for hours or possibly days) will then be scheduled. There may be some last-minute issues dealt with and there may not. If you are asking for days on the judge's calendar, the time between the status conference and the actual trial could be weeks or even months.

The last few weeks before any trial are times of great preparation. Subpoenas for witnesses and documents will be sent out and you will probably spend a great deal of time in your lawyer's office preparing with either your lawyer or the paralegal who has been assigned to your case. It's not unusual for the preparation for trial to take three to five times as long as the actual trial itself. You should be prepared for that sort of time investment as well as prepared for the legal fees that will be billed.

Your lawyer or the paralegal or legal assistant who is assisting your lawyer in preparing for the trial will inform you as to the location and time you should be available to start the trial. They will probably tell you not to bring your telephone or to turn it off before you actually walk into the courthouse. You will probably be instructed as to what to wear and how to prepare yourself personally for the hours or days of testimony that you're about to start on. If you have trouble sitting for hours, you should discuss this with your attorney and talk about any cushions or back supports you may be able to bring the court to help you get through it. You should remember to bring your own pad of paper and a pen or two so that you can take notes during the duration of the trial. It will be important for you to be able to take these notes so that you can assist your attorney in getting through the evidence by the witnesses and the documents that are put into evidence. Most judges allow witnesses, lawyers, and anybody else who wants to bring water or soft drinks in the court to do so. Water is usually provided in court or may be available immediately outside of the courtroom in a water fountain. I have never known any judge who would allow food or anything other than breath mints to be eaten during the course of trial. If you have been instructed by your attorney to bring some documents or anything else to the courtroom that day, you should go over that list and make sure you have them all.

The courtroom assigned for your trial may be very small or very large depending on the preference of the judge. In jurisdictions where there is no jury in a custody case, the hearing room may be as small as a living room. In jurisdictions where a jury does decide a custody case, the hearing room may be full-sized including a separate space for the jury to sit.

The place where the judge sits is called "the bench." The bench will be either in the very front of the room or in some corner but will be placed in such a manner that all of the seats in the room can see it. In some jurisdictions, the bench is raised slightly but in all jurisdictions it will be the focus of the room. Most often, there will be a podium either directly in front of the bench or directly in front of the jury if there is to be one. You and your lawyer will sit at what is called "the counsel table." Your ex or co-parent will sit at a counsel table either to your left or to your right. In some courtrooms, these tables are identified as for the plaintiff or the defendant. In your jurisdiction that might be called petitioner and respondent. By this point you should know which you are. These "council tables" will usually be right in front of "the bench." You will be led into the room by the bailiff, most probably, and given an opportunity to sit down, settle in, and organize whatever papers or items you will need before the trial actually starts.

The court personnel will probably be as follows:

1. The judge. The judge will be sitting at the bench and will probably be wearing a black robe. The robe could be a different color and could be either plain or have some adornments according to the taste of the judge.

2. The court clerk. The clerk will sit some place very close to the judge. The court clerk is charged with bringing the official court file to and from the court room and possibly identifying and marking documents or items of evidence into the record. The court clerk also has the judge's calendar.

3. The bailiff. The bailiff is in charge of keeping order and protecting the judge. The bailiff can also be a person who might carry evidence or documents between the counsel table and the judge during the course of the trial in some jurisdictions. The bailiffs are generally in charge of escorting the jury in an out of the courtroom in jurisdictions that use juries. The bailiff may be the one who takes the jury to the jury room or who may take questions from the jury to the judge if they are necessary. In most jurisdictions, the bailiffs are armed. In some jurisdictions the bailiffs are deputy sheriffs and in others they may be constables or police officers.

4. The court reporter. The court reporter is the person who is assigned to take down verbatim everything that is said in court. The court reporter may be

either using a shorthand machine or some other approved electronic device that records everything that is said. In some cases and in some jurisdictions the court reporter may be the one to mark evidence to be received. The purpose of marking evidence is to keep an accurate track of the number and the identification of what the evidence is for future reference.

5. The jury. If a jury is authorized to hear custody cases in your jurisdiction, the jury will be in the room whenever evidence or testimony is given except in very narrow circumstances. The jury is usually chosen from registered voters in your jurisdiction. The number depends on the type of case.

6. The witnesses. The witnesses will probably appear one by one as they are called by the attorneys into the room to testify. As a rule, witnesses are not allowed to hear each other's testimony except in the case of professional witnesses like psychologists, psychiatrists, or custody evaluators. The rest of the witnesses who are not testifying will remain either in witness rooms provided by the court or in the hallway outside of the courtroom.

WHEN THE TRIAL ACTUALLY BEGINS

At this point, you will not be able to say anything to anyone other than your lawyer or the judge when he or she asks. You will not be able to speak to the witnesses or directly to the judge unless the judge asks you for a response or you are directed to as a witness. You will only be able to speak to your lawyer in a whisper or by the notes you write on a pad and give to him or her. You will not be able to speak to anyone but your lawyer except under the circumstances above, until the trial is over.

The judge will walk into the room and take his or her seat at the bench. Generally, a judge will ask a question of both lawyers before commencing anything else. The question could either be "Are both the plaintiff and the defendant ready?" Or it could be something like "Are there any matters we need to take up before we begin?" If there are any last-minute matters that need to be dealt with, this is the point when the lawyers will bring them up to the judge. Last-minute matters can include unavailable witnesses, possibly a witness who may not be able to get there until later, any time constraints by either one of the lawyers that may have come up at the last minute, or any other unforeseen circumstances that have occurred in the last hours or days before the trial. Usually, these are dealt with fairly quickly. I have to warn you here, though, that I have seen trials that have been scheduled for months get continued at this point because of a lawyer or witness who is unavoidably unavailable due to no fault of anyone. In my practice, I have seen a lawyer who had an obvious fever and was completely unable to try the case come to court and ask for a delay. I have seen trials delayed because the judge was sick and, in one case, because the judge was in the Army Reserve and his unit had been deployed over the weekend. In one of my cases, my client, who was a Major in the active Army and a helicopter pilot was deployed during the invasion of Panama over the weekend and had been unable to call anyone to tell us of the deployment. I learned of it in the newspaper. I tell you these things because it's not impossible that after having waited for months you may get to the courthouse and have to wait for more months.

Either of the attorneys may at this point make oral motions to the court such as a request to "invoke the rule." "The rule" that they're talking about is the "rule of sequestration." This is not the sequestration you hear about in Congress but the rule of sequestration that applies to witnesses. The rule of sequestration maintains that all witnesses should be prohibited from speaking to each other about their testimony either before or after they testify, and they may not tell each other what questions are asked or what is occurring in the courtroom. This rule is very commonly invoked before the beginning of any trial and you should not attach any special meaning to it other than a desire on the part of one attorney or the other to keep the witnesses from talking to each other. The witnesses will probably be brought into court and explained the rule of sequestration before the trial gets underway if it is in fact invoked. A violation of the rule of sequestration can involve anything from a stern warning from the judge to defining a mistrial in the worst case scenario. If a mistrial is found, the judge will stop the trial, dismiss the parties and the witnesses, and the trial will have to begin again, possibly at a later date.

If there are no last-minute problems and everything is ready to proceed, the judge may "swear in" all of the witnesses (if the case is going to be short or if the number of witnesses will be small) or may simply look at the plaintiff's attorney and ask if he or she has any opening statements. If the plaintiff's attorney (sometimes known as the petitioner) makes an opening statement, generally the defendant's (respondent) attorney will also make an opening statement. The opening statement is a brief synopsis of what the attorney expects the witnesses and evidence to show to the court. The statement by the attorney is not evidence but is only given to let the judge know where the testimony will be going and what is expected of the testimony and evidence.

If the lawyers choose to give an opening statement, they will be allowed a certain amount of time to do it. At the close of both opening statements, or if the lawyers choose not to give opening statements, the judge will then look at the plaintiff's attorney and say "Call your first witness." This is when the trial truly begins.

Witnesses will be called in the order that the attorney who is calling them has decided is most effective and advantageous. Sometimes, witnesses with very little to say or witnesses who can be called for only one or two questions will be called first no matter what the importance of their testimony. This may not be true in all circumstances, but in most circumstances lawyers will try to get quick witnesses out of the way first. This is solely for the convenience of the witness. There are circumstances, however, when a quick witness may have very important testimony that can only become understandable after another or some other witnesses of testify. In that case the quick witness must wait.

The witnesses and evidence will generally be brought in according to the order in which they were listed on the *pretrial* statements we talked about before. These are the statements and schedules of evidence that were given to the judge and exchanged by the attorneys at the status conference or the pretrial conference where the trial was scheduled. There are circumstances where the documents, evidence, and witnesses may be called out of order and it's not terribly unusual for that to happen. You should really attach no significance to the fact that a witness or piece of evidence came into the record out of order. Some witnesses will be called upon to identify evidence and some will just be testifying from their memory. Witnesses are only allowed to testify as to what they saw, heard, smelled, or tasted. They may not guess or give opinions unless they are asked to and the judge has authorized them to make a guess or give an opinion. Generally, the judge will not ask them to and it is fairly unusual if they do.

The judge will make a specific ruling on the admissibility of each piece of evidence, document, or the testimony of each witness based on the rules of evidence. For example, there could be an objection to a witness testifying about what he heard someone else say as being *hearsay*. The witnesses are not allowed to testify about what they heard some third party say outside of the courtroom except in the case of expert witnesses and that is only when they are using these out-of-court statements to form their opinions. There may be objections during the course of the trial that go to the relevance or materiality of a piece of evidence. Usually, the judge has to make a determination on each of these as they happen. You should not attach any specific importance to each individual ruling or to any trend you might see happening in the rulings. For example, it generally doesn't mean much that the judge is ruling against your lawyer on evidence matters. Likewise, it ordinarily doesn't mean very much the judge is ruling with your lawyer on these items either. There may be significant and heated arguments sometimes about the admissibility of evidence. The only person who can explain why there is argument or the importance of the argument is your lawyer. Remember, during the course of the trial, you should never try to engage in any long discussions with your lawyer except outside of the courtroom. Your lawyer is trying to listen to what's going on at all times and can't very well do that if you are talking in his or her ear. If what you have to say is very important, you can ask your lawyer to get a break in the trial from the judge.

Earlier we talked about evidence that had been agreed upon by the attorneys coming in without someone to identify or authenticate it. There may be a time, and it usually occurs at the beginning of testimony or at the very end, when the attorneys ask the court to receive those certain pieces of evidence that they need to come in without the witness to authenticate them. There may be a very few or quite a few of these types of admissions.

The evidence may go on for hours or even days. I have seen custody and visitation trials that went on for weeks.

Each witness called will be asked questions by the lawyer calling him or her. After the lawyer who calls the witness is finished with the questioning, the other lawyer will be allowed to ask questions of the witness also. Usually, it will only be just the two sets of questions allowed. There are some circumstances where the lawyer who called the witness will be allowed to ask a few more questions but it's kind of unusual. The judge may also ask the witness a few questions also but that is pretty rare.

When all of the witnesses have finished testifying and all of the evidence has been admitted into the record and observed by the judge, there will be time allowed for closing statements by the attorneys. These are similar to the opening statements we talked about earlier. Each lawyer will be given an opportunity to talk for a certain amount of time to sum up the testimony and evidence that has come into the trial. In the case of custody and visitation matters, this is very probably where the lawyers will go through the items listed in Chapter 5 and try to draw the best references they can and the best interpretation of the evidence they can to make you the winner.

After all of the evidence is in and the lawyers have finished their closing arguments, the judge will charge the jury (give them their final instructions) or he or she will begin the deliberation phase of the trial. Whether there is a jury or the case has been tried by a judge, this is the time that either of them will think about what they have heard and try to make a decision as to what to do. The time for deliberations is up to the judge or jury actually doing the deliberating. It may be minutes, hours, or days. In any event, when they are finished, the result will be announced and the trial phase will be over. At that point, you will know if your preparation and presentation of your evidence has paid off or not.

If you read *Divorce and Conquer*, you know that this may not be the end. There can be a considerable degree or wrangling and argument about the wording of the final judgment and maybe even some adjustment of the language contained in it.

There is also the appeals process. I'm not going into that too much here, but in short, it is the process you can take when you or your lawyer thinks the judge has made a mistake. It's a long, arduous, and expensive process and should only be undertaken when the mistake by the judge is so bad that it is simple to see and has the ability to ruin your life or the lives of the kids. The appeal process takes the case and the case file before a panel of other judges who decide if the judge made a mistake in the first place and what to do about it after that. The chances of success in the appeal process are about one in seven so you really have to think about what you're doing before you start.

11

Modifications of Custody and Visitation Orders

SUBSTANTIAL CHANGES IN CIRCUMSTANCES

Substantial changes in circumstances are the threshold questions that must be proven in any modification of a custody and visitation order. In the vast majority of states, there must be a substantial change in circumstances in order to change or modify any order issued by a competent court. **All** custody and visitation orders can be changed upon proper proof, sometimes "in the best interests of the child(ren)" and sometimes "to avoid harm or detriment to the children."

First, the court that issued the original order setting custody and visitation will be the same court to modify it if it becomes necessary. You'll have to go back and look at the UCCJEA rules in Chapter 2 concerning parents who have left the jurisdiction and children who have left the jurisdiction if you have questions that involve changed jurisdiction circumstances, but, for the most part, the court that issued the original order will be the court that issues the order modifying it.

Many people are of the opinion that a custody and visitation order may not be modified by agreement of the parties. Let me dispel that myth right now. If you and your co-parent come to an agreement with regard to modification of your existing custody and visitation order and can show two things, (1) a substantial change in circumstances and, (2) that the best interest of the child will be served by the modification, you can change an existing order to fit the circumstances as they are currently. My experience is that the necessity for both the substantial change and the best interest of the children are somewhat relaxed when the parties agree to the changes. For the most part, judges will not interfere with the agreements of the parents unless the agreement on its face has some problem.

A substantial change in circumstances is something that is a little bit difficult to identify or define. It **cannot** be a fact that was known to the parties (and in some cases should have been known) at the time of the original final judgment. It must be something entirely new that has occurred since the entry of the final judgment. For example, if one parent had an existing problem with prescription drugs at the time of the entry of the final judgment and the other contesting parent knew about this problem, this could not be used as a substantial change in circumstances. However, given the same set of facts, if that parent had moved on to illegal drugs such as heroin or cocaine, this may be used as a substantial change in circumstances to modify a custody or visitation order.

As I indicated above, the change must be in the best interests of the child as well. The best interest of the child will always be served if it promotes a rich and continuing relationship with both the custodial parent and the visiting parent. Most state statutes require a shared responsibility custody order to be built-in to all custody and visitation schemes. This requires an active participation on the part of both parents. The best interest of the child may be served in some circumstances simply by one or the other of the parent's success in business or increased ability to provide for the child or participate in the child's life.

The change in circumstances must be truly substantial. For example, if one parent lives fifteen miles away from the other parent at the time of the issuance of the final judgment but moves seventeen miles away subsequent to the entry of final judgment, it's doubtful this would be called a substantial change unless the additional two miles caused that parent to move into a different country. Given the same set of circumstances, however, if the moving parent went from fifteen miles away to sixty miles away, this may be called a substantial change in circumstances because of the logistics of custody change and transportation. A parent who lives sixty miles away would find it difficult to attend the child's sporting events, doctor visits, or other events that would be fairly easy for a parent who lives fifteen miles away.

It's somewhat difficult for the parent who brings about a substantial change in circumstances voluntarily to ask for a change in a custody or visitation order. An involuntary change in circumstances is much more likely to result in the change in the custody or visitation order which may be required or desired. Let me give you an example. A parent who has a job as a machinist voluntarily changes her place of employment. The change in employment causes her to move sixty miles away from the co-parent. The change in the place of employment is a purely lateral change and does not increase or improve the financial situation of the parent who is moving. It would be very difficult for this parent to get any change in the custody and visitation order to increase visitation perhaps or to get help from the other parent and transportation of the child. If you change the facts slightly, however, the result could be different. Let's say the machinist changes her employment because instead of working the night shift for $15 an hour, by moving sixty miles away she could change to the day shift and make $25 an hour. Obviously, moving sixty miles away from where the child lives or where the child visits would still be a substantial but voluntary change. Even though the change would be voluntary on the part of the moving parent, the court **could** find that the move to the day shift and the $10 an hour increase in pay could be a significant benefit to the child and could find the substantial change in circumstances (although voluntary) to be in the best interests of the child and modify the custody or visitation order to fit the new circumstances. The best interest of the child would be served by this change because the machinist parent would now be able to enjoy some after-school events and provide a better life for the child because of the $400 week increase in pay.

You will have to discuss your changes with your attorney so that you and he or she can decide whether to bring an action for modification based on your facts.

We cannot discuss all of the potential changes in circumstances that may bring about a desire or need to change a final court order. Examples of what are and are not substantial changes would take volumes and complete law practices are made up of these things. The first decision has to be made by you and you are the one who's going to have to decide whether or not the change in your life or the change in your ex's life is something big enough that you're willing to go to court over. Second, you have to decide whether the change will affect the best interest of the child(ren) to such an extent that you're willing to go to court again.

Change substantial enough to modify the custodial parent designation must be enormous. It has to be large enough and serious enough to convince a judge to undo what he or she has already decided or undo what the parents have agreed to in the past. Some jurisdictions hold that to modify a custody and visitation scheme, the court must find that to leave it in place would somehow injure the child.

WHEN A CUSTODIAL PARENT INTENDS TO LEAVE THE JURISDICTION OF THE COURT

When a custodial parent, or anyone who is standing in the place of a parent, intends to move a significant distance away from the visiting parent, there can be strict and lengthy hurdles in his or her way. A significant number of states now have a specific procedure that must be followed in order to give the visiting parent adequate notice that the custodial parent will be moving and give them an opportunity to resist or attempt to block the move because of the impact it will have on the relationship between the visiting parent and the child and the difficulty in logistics and transportation the move will cause.

Relocation in this situation means that the custodial parent, or that person acting as the custodial parent by agreement or court order, is moving his or her permanent residence more than sixty miles away from his or her current residence with the intention of making permanent residence in that place. Some statutes only require a move of fifty miles. In this situation, you will notice that it is not only the parents but someone acting as parents and having primary residential care over the child or children. This may include the grandparents, uncles, and aunts or anyone else who may have an order or orders identifying them as a primary residential parent.

If the move has the consent of the non-custodial parent, there may still be a procedure that must be followed. The typical language required for an agreement for consensual relocation by custodial parent generally includes the following:

1. It must reflect consent to the relocation.

2. It must define an access or time-sharing schedule for the nonrelocating parent and any other persons who are entitled to access or time-sharing.

3. It must describe, if necessary, any transportation arrangements related to access or time-sharing.

If there is an existing cause of action, judgment, or decree of record pertaining to the child's residence or a time-sharing schedule, the parties shall seek ratification of the agreement by court order without the necessity of an evidentiary hearing unless a hearing is requested, in writing, by one or more of the parties to the agreement within ten days after the date the agreement is filed with the court. If a hearing is not timely requested, it shall be presumed that the relocation is in the best interest of the child and the court may ratify the agreement without an evidentiary hearing.

If there is not an agreement to allow the relocation, the petition must be filed for modification of the final judgment to include the relocation of the primary residential parent and the following steps may be required:

A. The petition to relocate must be signed under oath or affirmation under penalty of perjury and include:

1. A description of the location of the intended new residence, including the state, city, and specific physical address, if known.

2. The mailing address of the intended new residence, if not the same as the physical address, if known.

3. The home telephone number of the intended new residence, if known.

4. The date of the intended move or proposed relocation.

5. A detailed statement of the specific reasons for the proposed relocation. If one of the reasons is based upon a job offer that has been reduced to writing, the written job offer must be attached to the petition.

6. A proposal for the revised post-relocation schedule for access and time-sharing together with a proposal for the post-relocation transportation arrangements necessary to effectuate time-sharing with the child. Absent the existence of a current, valid order abating, terminating, or restricting access or time-sharing or other good cause predating the petition, failure to comply with this provision renders the petition to relocate legally insufficient.

7. Substantially the following statement, in all capital letters and in the same size type, or larger, as the type in the remainder of the petition:

A RESPONSE TO THE PETITION OBJECTING TO RELOCATION MUST BE MADE IN WRITING, FILED

WITH THE COURT, AND SERVED ON THE PARENT OR OTHER PERSON SEEKING TO RELOCATE WITHIN 20 DAYS AFTER SERVICE OF THIS PETITION TO RELOCATE. IF YOU FAIL TO TIMELY OBJECT TO THE RELOCATION, THE RELOCATION WILL BE ALLOWED, UNLESS IT IS NOT IN THE BEST INTERESTS OF THE CHILD, WITHOUT FURTHER NOTICE AND WITHOUT A HEARING.

B. The petition to relocate must be served on the other parent and on every other person entitled to access to and time-sharing with the child. If there is a pending court action regarding the child, service of process may be according to court rule.

C. A parent or other person seeking to relocate has a continuing duty to provide current and updated information required by this section when that information becomes known.

D. If the other parent and any other person entitled to access to or time-sharing with the child fails to timely file a response objecting to the petition to relocate, it is presumed that the relocation is in the best interest of the child and that the relocation should be allowed, and the court shall, absent good cause, enter an order specifying that the order is entered as a result of the failure to respond to the petition and adopting the access and time-sharing schedule and transportation arrangements contained in the petition. The order may be issued in an expedited manner without the necessity of an evidentiary hearing. If a response is timely filed, the parent or other person may not relocate and must proceed to a temporary hearing or trial and obtain court permission to relocate.

E. Relocating the child without complying with the requirements of this subsection subjects the party in violation to contempt and other proceedings to compel the return of the child and may be taken into account by the court in any initial or post-judgment action seeking a determination or modification of the parenting plan or the access or time-sharing schedule as:

1. A factor in making a determination regarding the relocation of a child.

2. A factor in determining whether the parenting plan or the access or time-sharing schedule should be modified.

3. A basis for ordering the temporary or permanent return of the child.

(Copied from Florida Statute 61.13001)

There may be other requirements in your state or jurisdiction. These are copied from Florida because they seem to be fairly standard and restrictive. You will have to consult with your attorney about the applicability and possible further requirements for a custodial parent to remove a child from their home.

The judge will still have to find a substantial benefit to the child in order to allow the move. Usually the moving parent will have a significantly increased duty with regard to transportation and extended visitation for the parent left in the original jurisdiction. This is not a simple proposition and will require much preparation.

Once your threshold has been met (significant change of circumstances), the trial court will have to go on to the second phase and determine that the child's best interest will be served by the change.

The change or modification can be to almost anything having to do with the custody and visitation arrangement. It can be a change of custody itself, moving the child from the home of one parent to another, a change in the visitation schedule, either expanding it or making it smaller, or a change in logistics and transportation. Once the judge has found that a substantial change has occurred warranting a modification, almost anything can happen.

If your goal is a change in either custody or visitation, you should be prepared to present a new parenting plan reflecting what your goals are. These should be presented to your attorney well in advance of any hearing on this so that he or she can assist you in clarifying and perfecting the parenting plan before it is actually presented to the judge for consideration.

TAKEAWAYS

Changing or modifying a custody and visitation schedule is as difficult as and sometimes even more difficult than the original custody fight itself. There can be significant feelings of betrayal and rekindling of anger involved in a case like this.

All of the discovery techniques including oral, written, and documentary are available during the pretrial portions of these cases. There can be just as many motion hearings and temporary hearings involved in one of these as there are in original proceeding. The cost can be as much or more than an original proceeding. The point is, make sure that your change in circumstances is significant before you undertake one of these and make sure that you are resolved to complete it once you start.

Appendix

INSTRUCTIONS FOR FLORIDA SUPREME COURT APPROVED FAMILY LAW FORM 12.902(d), UNIFORM CHILD CUSTODY JURISDICTION AND ENFORCEMENT ACT (UCCJEA) AFFIDAVIT (12/10)

When should this form be used?

This form should be used in any case involving custody of, visitation with, or time-sharing with any minor child(ren). This **affidavit** is **required** even if the custody of, visitation, or time-sharing with the minor child(ren) are not in dispute.

This form should be typed or printed in black ink. After completing this form, you should sign the form before a **notary public** or **deputy clerk**. You should then **file** the original with the **clerk of the circuit court** in the county where the petition was filed and keep a copy for your records.

What should I do next?

A copy of this form must be mailed or hand delivered to the other party in your case, if it is not served on him or her with your initial papers.

Where can I look for more information?

Before proceeding, you should read General Information for Self–Represented Litigants found at the beginning of these forms. The words that are in **bold underline** in these instructions are defined there. For further information, see sections 61.501-61.542, Florida Statutes.

Special notes...

Chapter 2008-61, Laws of Florida, effective October 1, 2008, eliminated such terms as custodial parent, noncustodial parent, primary residential parent, secondary residential parent, and visitation from Chapter 61, Florida Statutes. Instead, parents are to develop a Parenting Plan that includes, among other things, their time-sharing schedule with the minor child(ren). If the parents cannot agree, a parenting plan will be established by the Court. However, because the UCCJEA uses the terms custody and visitation, they are included in this form.

If you are the petitioner in an injunction for protection against domestic violence case and you have filed **a Request for Confidential Filing of Address**, Florida Supreme Court Approved Family Law Form 12.980(h), you should write confidential in any space on this form that would require you to write the address where you are currently living.

Remember, a person who is NOT an attorney is called a nonlawyer. If a nonlawyer helps you fill out these forms, that person must give you a copy of a **Disclosure from Nonlawyer**, Florida Family Law Rules of Procedure Form 12.900(a), before he or she helps you. A nonlawyer helping you fill out these forms

also **must** put his or her name, address, and telephone number on the bottom of the last page of every form he or she helps you complete.

Instructions for Florida Supreme Court Approved Family Law Form 12.902(d), Uniform Child Custody Jurisdiction   and Enforcement Act (UCCJEA) Affidavit (12/10)

IN THE CIRCUIT COURT OF THE _____ JUDICIAL CIRCUIT,
IN AND FOR _____ COUNTY, FLORIDA

Case No.: _____
Division: _____

_____,
Petitioner,

and

_____,
Respondent.

UNIFORM CHILD CUSTODY JURISDICTION AND ENFORCEMENT ACT (UCCJEA) AFFIDAVIT

I, *{full legal name}* _____, being sworn, certify that the following statements are true:

1. The number of minor child(ren) subject to this proceeding is _____. The name, place of birth, birth date, and sex of each child; the present address, periods of residence, and places where each child has lived **within the past five (5) years**; and the name, present address, and relationship to the child of each person with whom the child has lived during that time are:

THE FOLLOWING INFORMATION IS TRUE ABOUT CHILD # __1__:

Child's Full Legal Name: _____
Place of Birth: _____ Date of Birth: _____ Sex: _____

Child's Residence for the past 5 years:

Dates (From/To)	Address (including city and state) where child lived	Name and present address of person child lived with	Relationship to child
_____/present*			
___/___			
___/___			
___/___			
___/___			

Florida Supreme Court Approved Family Law Form 12.902(d), Uniform Child Custody Jurisdiction and Enforcement Act (UCCJEA) Affidavit (12/10)

___/___			

* If you are the petitioner in an injunction for protection against domestic violence case and you have filedaRequest for Confidential Filing of Address, Florida Supreme Court Approved Family Law Form 12.980(h), you should write confidential in any space on this form that would require you to enter the address where you are currently living.

THE FOLLOWING INFORMATION IS TRUE ABOUT CHILD # ____:

Child's Full Legal Name: _____

Place of Birth: _____ Date of Birth: _____ Sex: _____

Child's Residence for the past 5 years:

Dates (From/To)	Address (including city and state) where child lived	Name and present address of person child lived with	Relationship to child
_____/present			
___/___			
___/___			
___/___			
___/___			
___/___			

THE FOLLOWING INFORMATION IS TRUE ABOUT CHILD # ____:

Child's Full Legal Name: _____

Place of Birth: _____ Date of Birth: _____ Sex: _____

Child's Residence for the past 5 years:

Dates (From/To)	Address (including city and state) where child lived	Name and present address of person child lived with	Relationship to child
_____/present			
___/___			

Florida Supreme Court Approved Family Law Form 12.902(d), Uniform Child Custody Jurisdiction and Enforcement Act (UCCJEA) Affidavit (12/10)

__/__			
__/__			
__/__			
__/__			

2. **Participation in custody or time-sharing proceeding(s):**
[**Choose only one**]
☐ I HAVE NOT participated as a party, witness, or in any capacity in any other litigation or custody proceeding in this or any other state, concerning custody of or time-sharing with a child subject to this proceeding.
☐ I HAVE participated as a party, witness, or in any capacity in any other litigation or custody proceeding in this or another state, concerning custody of or time-sharing with a child subject to this proceeding. Explain:
   a. Name of each child: _____
   b. Type of proceeding: _____
   c. Court and state: _____
   d. Date of court order or judgment (if any): _____

3. **Information about custody or time-sharing proceeding(s):**
[**Choose only one**]
☐ I HAVE NO INFORMATION of any custody or time-sharing proceeding pending in a court of this or any other state concerning a child subject to this proceeding.
☐ I HAVE THE FOLLOWING INFORMATION concerning a custody or time-sharing proceeding pending in a court of this or another state concerning a child subject to this proceeding, other than set out in item 2. Explain:
   a. Name of each child: _____
   b. Type of proceeding: _____
   c. Court and state: _____
   d. Date of court order or judgment (if any): _____

4. **Persons not a party to this proceeding:**
[**Choose only one**]
☐ I DO NOT KNOW OF ANY PERSON not a party to this proceeding who has physical custody or claims to have custody, visitation or time-sharing with respect to any child subject to this proceeding.
☐ I KNOW THAT THE FOLLOWING NAMED PERSON(S) not a party to this proceeding has (have) physical custody or claim(s) to have custody, visitation, or time-sharing with respect to any child subject to this proceeding:
   a. Name and address of person: _____

_____
☐ has physical custody ☐ claims custody rights ☐ claims visitation or time-sharing
Name of each child: _____

Florida Supreme Court Approved Family Law Form 12.902(d), Uniform Child Custody Jurisdiction and Enforcement Act (UCCJEA) Affidavit (12/10)

b. Name and address of person: _____

_____

(☐) has physical custody (☐) claims custody rights (☐) claims visitation. or time-sharing
Name of each child: _____

c. Name and address of person: _____

_____

(☐) has physical custody (☐) claims custody rights (☐) claims visitation or time-sharing
Name of each child: _____

5. **Knowledge of prior child support proceedings:**
   [Choose only one]
   ☐ The child(ren) described in this affidavit are NOT subject to existing child support order(s) in this or any state or territory.
   ☐ The child(ren) described in this affidavit are subject to the following existing child support order(s):
   a. Name of each child:
   b. Type of proceeding:
   c. Court and address:
   d. Date of court order/judgment (if any):
   e. Amount of child support paid and by whom: _____

6. **I acknowledge that I have a continuing duty to advise this Court of any custody, visitation or time-sharing, child support, or guardianship proceeding (including dissolution of marriage, separate maintenance, child neglect, or dependency) concerning the child(ren) in this state or any other state about which information is obtained during this proceeding.**

I certify that a copy of this document was [**Choose only one**] (☐) mailed (☐) faxed and mailed (☐) hand delivered to the person(s) listed below on *{date}* _____.

Other party or his/her attorney:
Name: _____
Address: _____
City, State, Zip: _____
Fax Number: _____

Florida Supreme Court Approved Family Law Form 12.902(d), Uniform Child Custody Jurisdiction and Enforcement Act (UCCJEA) Affidavit (12/10)

I understand that I am swearing or affirming under oath to the truthfulness of the claims made in this affidavit and that the punishment for knowingly making a false statement includes fines and/or imprisonment.

Dated: _____

                     _____

                     Signature of Party
                     Printed Name: _____
                     Address: _____
                     City, State, Zip: _____
                     Telephone Number: _____
                     Fax Number: _____

STATE OF FLORIDA
COUNTY OF _____

Sworn to or affirmed and signed before me on _____ by _____.

                     _____
                     NOTARY PUBLIC or DEPUTY CLERK

                     _____
                     [Print, type, or stamp commissioned name of notary or clerk.]

☐ Personally known
☐ Produced identification
    Type of identification produced

IF A NONLAWYER HELPED YOU FILL OUT THIS FORM, HE/SHE MUST FILL IN THE BLANKS BELOW: [fill in **all** blanks]
I, *{full legal name and trade name of nonlawyer}* _____,
a nonlawyer, located at *{street}* _____, *{city}* _____,
{state} _____, *{phone}* _____, helped *{name}* _____,
who is the [**Choose only one**] ☐ petitioner or ☐ respondent, fill out this form.

Florida Supreme Court Approved Family Law Form 12.902(d), Uniform Child Custody Jurisdiction and Enforcement Act (UCCJEA) Affidavit (12/10)

About the Author

R. Ray Brooks has been a soldier, prosecutor and for the last thirty four years, a trial lawyer specializing in divorces and family law cases. During his career, he represented both men and women in cases involving custody and visitation, property divisions, and child support and alimony. He has been an invited seminar speaker and an accepted expert witness in the field of contested attorney's fees as well as a three time elected member of the family law section board of directors in Hillsborough County Florida. He is now the author of the three part "Conquering Divorce" series. Yes, he understands divorce on many levels being divorced himself. He now lives in Georgia with his wife and two dogs.

CPSIA information can be obtained at www.ICGtesting.com
Printed in the USA
LVOW08s1551040214

372300LV00002B/465/P

9 781611 530896